the
poetry
of
World
War I

the poetry of World War I

This edition published in 2018 by Arcturus Publishing Limited
26/27 Bickels Yard, 151–153 Bermondsey Street,
London SE1 3HA

AD006337UK

Printed in the UK

Contents

Introduction

While war has been used as a theme by poets throughout history, no conflict has ever been so closely linked with the literature of its age than World War I. The work produced between 1914 and 1918 includes some of the most moving poetry in English literature. It is a common misconception that these poets were all well-educated young men from privileged backgrounds, but included in this compelling collection are words written by artists, doctors, nurses, journalists, labourers, farmers and others too young to have embarked on their working lives as well as those educated at Eton College and Oxford University. There are poems by men and women, husbands, wives, sons and daughters, fighters and non-combatants alike. They were not all anti-war either; there were warmongers, jingoists, propagandists and even those looking for some excitement in their dull lives among them. The fact is that the English War Poets, of which the official registered number is an astonishing 2,225, were from all generations and all classes. Of course, it doesn't stop with them – some scholars estimate that there were three million war poems composed by German writers, too, as well as soldiers and members of the public in other countries such as Canada, the United States, France and Australia.

During the early summer of 1914, Europe was in a state of chaos with conflict looming ahead. The prevailing emotion across the continent was nationalistic, and when Britain declared war on Germany on 4 August a wave a patriotism swept across Britain. A great number of young men from all walks of life answered the nation's call to arms, not wanting to miss out on the 'fun' that they would have finishing the war by Christmas. But their hopes were soon dashed by the horrors they experienced on the Front Line – flea-ridden uniforms, ill-fitting boots, rat-infested trenches oozing with mud, freezing temperatures, no sleep because of the noise of bombardment and the ever-present threat of death.

The impact of these experiences hit everyone, officers and men alike. Soldiers were forbidden to write home with much detail for fear of giving away military information, so many put their thoughts into diaries, which could be kept in secret. Others wrote poetry and, as poems rely on interpretation rather than fact, their work bypassed any military censorship and made its way home to Blighty and further afield. And newspapers and magazines were only too keen to publish it. In turn, the words were read by children waiting for their fathers to come home, wives waiting for their husbands and parents waiting for news of their sons. In such a way, details of the conditions on the Western Front reached a public hungry for news about the conflict.

That poems such as 'In Flanders Field' by John McRae, 'The Soldier' by Rupert Brooke, 'My Boy Jack' by Rudyard Kipling, 'The Cenotaph' by Charlotte Mew and 'Dulce et Decorum Est' by Wilfred Owen, all included here, are still redolent for readers today is testament in part to the elemental subject matter and the emotions the words stir in us. So, too, the fact that many of the authors died as a consequence of their involvement in the war, such as Wilfred Owen, whose mother received notice of his death on 11 November 1918 – the same day that the conflict finally came to an end. But they also serve to explain the beginnings of the modern world. It is hard for us to imagine a 500-mile line of trenches or that millions of young men died in no man's land, hanging off barbed wire in a hail of machine-gun bullets, cannon fire or as a result of inhaling poisonous gas. After four years of this, and with nine million dead, the opposing forces were pretty much where they had been when they started.

It is in no small part thanks to the poets and the diary writers that the truth of this terrible conflict was revealed. When the fighting finally ceased, something had changed in human sensibility. From then on, no society would accept such pointless slaughter. Today, though almost all the witnesses of the war to end all wars have gone, the words left by the poets and other writers of the time still exert a strong hold on our imagination.

The Treasure

When colour goes home into the eyes,
And lights that shine are shut again,
With dancing girls and sweet birds' cries
Behind the gateways of the brain;
And that no-place which gave them birth, shall close
The rainbow and the rose:-

Still may Time hold some golden space
Where I'll unpack that scented store
Of song and flower and sky and face,
And count, and touch, and turn them o'er,
Musing upon them; as a mother who
Has watched her children all the rich day through,
Sits, quiet-handed, in the fading light,
When children sleep, ere night.

Rupert Brooke

War Sonnets

I. Peace

Now, God be thanked Who has matched us with His hour,
And caught our youth, and wakened us from sleeping
With hand made sure, clear eye, and sharpened power,
To turn, as swimmers into cleanness leaping,
Glad from a world grown old and cold and weary,
Leave the sick hearts that honour could not move,
And half-men, and their dirty songs and dreary,
And all the little emptiness of love!

Oh! we, who have known shame, we have found release
  there,
Where there's no ill, no grief, but sleep has mending,
Naught broken save this body, lost but breath;
Nothing to shake the laughing heart's long peace there
But only agony, and that has ending;
And the worst friend and enemy is but Death.

II. Safety

Dear! of all happy in the hour, most blest
He who has found our hid security,
Assured in the dark tides of the world at rest,
And heard our word, 'Who is so safe as we?'
We have found safety with all things undying,
The winds, and morning, tears of men and mirth,
The deep night, and birds singing, and clouds flying,
And sleep, and freedom, and the autumnal earth.
We have built a house that is not for Time's throwing.
We have gained a peace unshaken by pain for ever.
War knows no power. Safe shall be my going,

Secretly armed against all death's endeavour;
Safe though all safety's lost; safe where men fall;
And if these poor limbs die, safest of all.

III. The Dead

Blow out, you bugles, over the rich Dead!
There's none of these so lonely and poor of old,
But, dying, has made us rarer gifts than gold.
These laid the world away; poured out the red
Sweet wine of youth; gave up the years to be
Of work and joy, and that unhoped serene,
That men call age; and those who would have been,
Their sons, they gave, their immortality.

Blow, bugles, blow! They brought us, for our dearth,
Holiness, lacked so long, and Love, and Pain.
Honour has come back, as a king, to earth,
And paid his subjects with a royal wage;
And nobleness walks in our ways again;
And we have come into our heritage.

IV. The Dead

These hearts were woven of human joys and cares,
Washed marvellously with sorrow, swift to mirth.
The years had given them kindness. Dawn was theirs,
And sunset, and the colours of the earth.
These had seen movement, and heard music; known
Slumber and waking; loved; gone proudly friended;
Felt the quick stir of wonder; sat alone;

Touched flowers and furs and cheeks. All this is ended.
There are waters blown by changing winds to laughter

And lit by the rich skies, all day. And after,
Frost, with a gesture, stays the waves that dance
And wandering loveliness. He leaves a white
Unbroken glory, a gathered radiance,
A width, a shining peace, under the night.

V. The Soldier

If I should die, think only this of me:
That there's some corner of a foreign field
That is for ever England. There shall be
In that rich earth a richer dust concealed;
A dust whom England bore, shaped, made aware,
Gave, once, her flowers to love, her ways to roam,
A body of England's, breathing English air,
Washed by the rivers, blest by suns of home.

And think, this heart, all evil shed away,
A pulse in the eternal mind, no less
Gives somewhere back the thoughts by England given;
Her sights and sounds; dreams happy as her day;
And laughter, learnt of friends; and gentleness,
In hearts at peace, under an English heaven.

Rupert Brooke

Last Lines

I

Ah! Hate like this would freeze our human tears,
And stab the morning star:
Not it, not it commands and mourns and bears
The storm and bitter glory of red war.

II

To J.H.S.M., killed in action, March 13, 1915

O brother, I have sung no dirge for thee:
Nor for all time to come
Can song reveal my grief's infinity:
The menace of thy silence made me dumb.

R.W. Sterling

I Tracked a Dead Man
Down a Trench

I tracked a dead man down a trench,
I knew not he was dead.
They told me he had gone that way,
And there his foot-marks led.

The trench was long and close and curved,
It seemed without an end;
And as I threaded each new bay
I thought to see my friend.

I went there stooping to the ground,
For, should I raise my head,
Death watched to spring; and how should then
A dead man find the dead?

At last I saw his back. He crouched
As still as still could be,
And when I called his name aloud
He did not answer me.

The floor-way of the trench was wet
Where he was crouching dead:
The water of the pool was brown,
And round him it was red.

I stole up softly where he stayed
With head hung down all slack,
And on his shoulders laid my hands
And drew him gently back.

And then, as I had guessed, I saw
His head, and how the crown –
I saw then why he crouched so still,
And why his head hung down.

W.S.S. Lyon

Release

There is a healing magic in the night,
The breeze blows cleaner than it did by day,
Forgot the fever of the fuller light,
And sorrow sinks insensibly away
As if some saint a cool white hand did lay
Upon the brow, and calm the restless brain.
The moon looks down with pale unpassioned ray –
Sufficient for the hour is its pain.
Be still and feel the night that hides away earth's stain.
Be still and loose the sense of God in you,
Be still and send your soul into the all,
The vasty distance where the stars shine blue,
No longer antlike on the earth to crawl.
Released from time and sense of great or small,
Float on the pinions of the Night-Queen's wings;
Soar till the swift inevitable fall
Will drag you back into all the world's small things;
Yet for an hour be one with all escaped things.

Colwyn Philipps

Into Battle

(Flanders, April 1915)

The naked earth is warm with Spring,
And with green grass and bursting trees
Leans to the sun's gaze glorying,
And quivers in the sunny breeze;

And life is colour and warmth and light,
And a striving evermore for these;
And he is dead who will not fight;
And who dies fighting has increase.

The fighting man shall from the sun
Take warmth, and life from the glowing earth;
Speed with the light-foot winds to run,

And with the trees to newer birth;
And find, when fighting shall be done,
Great rest, and fullness after dearth.

All the bright company of Heaven
Hold him in their high comradeship,
The Dog-Star, and the Sisters Seven,
Orion's Belt and sworded hip.

The woodland trees that stand together,
They stand to him each one a friend;
They gently speak in the windy weather;
They guide to valley and ridge's end.

The kestrel hovering by day,
And the little owls that call by night,
Bid him be swift and keen as they,
As keen of ear, as swift of sight.

The blackbird sings to him, 'Brother, brother,
If this be the last song you shall sing,
Sing well, for you may not sing another;
Brother, sing.'

In dreary, doubtful, waiting hours,
Before the brazen frenzy starts,
The horses show him nobler powers;
O patient eyes, courageous hearts!

And when the burning moment breaks,
And all things else are out of mind,
And only joy of battle takes
Him by the throat, and makes him blind,

Through joy and blindness he shall know,
Not caring much to know, that still
Nor lead nor steel shall reach him, so
That it be not the Destined Will.

The thundering line of battle stands,
And in the air death moans and sings;
But Day shall clasp him with strong hands,
And Night shall fold him in soft wings.

Julian Grenfell

Prayer for Those on the Staff

Fighting in mud, we turn to Thee,
In these dread times of battle, Lord.
To keep us safe, if so may be,
From shrapnel, snipers, shell, and sword.

But not on us, for we are men
Of meaner clay, who fight in clay,
But on the Staff, the Upper Ten,
Depends the issue of the Day.

The Staff is working with its brains,
While we are sitting in the trench;
The Staff the universe ordains
(subject to Thee and General French).

God help the Staff – especially
The young ones, many of them sprung
From our high aristocracy;
Their task is hard, and they are young.

O Lord, who mad'st all things to be,
And madest some things very good,
Please keep the extra A.D.C.
From horrid scenes, and sight of blood.

See that his eggs are newly laid,
Not tinged as some of them – with green;
And let no nasty draughts invade
The windows of his Limousine.

When he forgets to buy the bread,
When there are no more minerals,
Preserve his smooth well-oilèd head
From wrath of caustic Generals.

O Lord, who mad'st all things to be,
And hatest nothing thou has made,
Please keep the extra A.D.C
Out of the sun and in the shade.

Julian Grenfell

To Germany

You are blind like us. Your hurt no man designed,
And no man claimed the conquest of your land.
But gropers both, through fields of thought confined,
We stumble and we do not understand.
You only saw your future bigly planned,
And we the tapering paths of our own mind,
And in each other's dearest ways we stand,
And hiss and hate. And the blind fight the blind.

When it is peace, then we may view again
With new-won eyes each other's truer form,
And wonder. Grown more loving-kind and warm
We'll grasp firm hands and laugh at the old pain,
When it is peace. But until peace, the storm,
The darkness and the thunder and the rain.

Charles Hamilton Sorley

All the Hills and Vales Along

All the hills and vales along
Earth is bursting into song,
And the singers are the chaps
Who are going to die perhaps.
O sing, marching men,
Till the valleys ring again.
Give your gladness to earth's keeping,
So be glad, when you are sleeping.

Cast away regret and rue,
Think what you are marching to.
Little live, great pass.
Jesus Christ and Barabbas
Were found the same day.
This died, that went his way.
So sing with joyful breath,
For why, you are going to death.
Teeming earth will surely store
All the gladness that you pour.

Earth that never doubts nor fears,
Earth that knows of death, not tears,
Earth that bore with joyful ease
Hemlock for Socrates,
Earth that blossomed and was glad
'Neath the cross that Christ had,
Shall rejoice and blossom too
When the bullet reaches you.
Wherefore, men marching
On the road to death, sing!

Pour your gladness on earth's head,
So be merry, so be dead.

From the hills and valleys earth
Shouts back the sound of mirth,
Tramp of feet and lilt of song
Ringing all the road along.
All the music of their going,
Ringing swinging glad song-throwing,
Earth will echo still, when foot
Lies numb and voice mute.
On, marching men, on
To the gates of death with song.
Sow your gladness for earth's reaping,
So you may be glad, though sleeping.
Strew your gladness on earth's bed,
So be merry, so be dead.

Charles Hamilton Sorley

When You See Millions of the Mouthless Dead

When you see millions of the mouthless dead
Across your dreams in pale battalions go,
Say not soft things as other men have said,
That you'll remember. For you need not so.
Give them not praise. For, deaf, how should they know
It is not curses heaped on each gashed head?
Nor tears. Their blind eyes see not your tears flow.
Nor honour. It is easy to be dead.
Say only this, 'They are dead.' Then add thereto,
'Yet many a better one has died before.'
Then, scanning all the o'ercrowded mass, should you
Perceive one face that you loved heretofore,
It is a spook. None wears the face you knew.
Great death has made all his for evermore.

Charles Hamilton Sorley

From Dolores

Six of us lay in a Dugout
At ease, with our limbs astretch,
And worshipped a feminine picture
Cut from a week-old *Sketch*.
We gazed at her Silken Stockings,
We studied her Cupid bow,
And we thought of the Suppers we used to buy
And the girls that we used to know.
And we all, in our several fashions,
Paid toll to the Lady's charms,
From the man of a hundred passions
To the Subaltern child-in-arms.
Never the sketch of a master
So jealously kept and prized,
Never a woman of flesh and blood
So truly idealized.
And because of her slender ankle,
And her coiffure – distinctly French –
We called her 'La Belle Dolores' –
'The Vivandière of the Trench.'

Cyril Horne

Love of Life

Reach out thy hands, thy spirit's hands, to me
And pluck the youth, the magic from my heart –
Magic of dreams whose sensibility
Is plumed like the light; visions that start
Mad pressure in the blood; desire that thrills
The soul with mad delight: to yearning wed
All slothfulness of life; draw from its bed
The soul of dawn across the twilight hills.
Reach out thy hands, O spirit, till I feel
That I am fully thine; for I shall live
In the proud consciousness that thou dost give,
And if thy twilight fingers round me steal
And draw me unto death – thy votary
Am I, O Life; reach out thy hands to me!

J.W. Streets

Lines Before Going

Soon is the night of our faring to regions unknown,
There not to flinch at the challenge suddenly thrown
By the great process of Being – daily to see
The utmost that life has of horror, and yet to be
Calm and the masters of fear. Aware that the soul
Lives as a part and alone for the weal of the whole,
So shall the mind be free from the pain of regret,
Vain and enfeebling, firm in each venture, and yet
Brave not as those who despair, but keen to maintain,
Though not assured, hope in beneficent pain.
Hope that the truth of the world is not what appears,
Hope in the triumph of man for the price of his tears.

Alexander Robertson

Ave, Mater – atque Vale

The deathless mother, grey and battle-scarred,
Lies in the sanctuary of stately trees,
Where the deep Northern night is saffron starred
Above her head, and thro' the dusk she sees
God's shadowy fortress keep unsleeping guard.

From her full breast we drank of joy and mirth
And gave to her a boy's unreasoned heart,
Wherein Time's fullness was to bring to birth
Such passionate allegiance that to part
Seemed like the passing of all light on earth.

Now on the threshold of a man's estate,
With a new depth of love akin to pain
I ask thy blessing, while I dedicate
My life and sword, with promise to maintain
Thine ancient honour yet inviolate.

Last night dream-hearted in the Abbey's spell
We stood to sing old Simeon's passing hymn,
When sudden splendour of the sunset fell
Full on my eyes, and passed and left all dim –
At once a summons and a deep farewell.

I am content – our life is but a trust
From the great hand of God, and if I keep
The immortal Treasure clean of mortal rust

Against His claim, 'tis well and let me sleep
Among the not dishonourable dust.

W.N. Hodgson

Release

A leaping wind from England,
The skies without a stain,
Clean cut against the morning
Slim poplars after rain,
The foolish noise of sparrows
And starlings in a wood –
After the grime of battle
We know that these are good.

Death whining down from heaven,
Death roaring from the ground,
Death stinking in the nostril,
Death shrill in every sound,

Doubting we charged and conquered –
Hopeless we struck and stood;
Now when the fight is ended
We know that it was good.

We that have seen the strongest
Cry like a beaten child,
The sanest eyes unholy,
The cleanest hands defiled,
We that have known the heart-blood
Less than the lees of wine,
We that have seen men broken,
We know that man is divine.

W. N. Hodgson

Before Action

By all the glories of the day
And the cool evening's benison,
By that last sunset touch that lay
Upon the hills when day was done,
By beauty lavishly outpoured
And blessings carelessly received,
By all the days that I have lived
Make me a soldier, Lord.

By all of man's hopes and fears,
And all the wonders poets sing,
The laughter of unclouded years,
And every sad and lovely thing;
By the romantic ages stored
With high endeavour that was his,
By all his mad catastrophes
Make me a man, O Lord.

I, that on my unfamiliar hill
Saw with uncomprehending eyes
A hundred of Thy sunsets spill
Their fresh and sanguine sacrifice,
Ere the sun swings his noonday sword
Must say good-bye to all of this; –
By all delights that I shall miss,
Help me to die, O Lord.

W. N. Hodgson

Resurgam

Exiled afar from youth and happy love,
If Death should ravish my fond spirit hence
I have no doubt but, like a homing dove,
It would return to its dear residence,
And through a thousand stars find out the road
Back into earthly flesh that was its loved abode.

Alan Seeger

The Aisne, 1914–15

We first saw fire on the tragic slopes
Where the flood-tide of France's early gain,
Big with wrecked promise and abandoned hopes,
Broke in a surf of blood along the Aisne.

The charge her heroes left us, we assumed,
What, dying, they reconquered, we preserved,
In the chill trenches, harried, shelled, entombed,
Winter came down on us, but no man swerved.

Winter came down on us. The low clouds, torn
In the stark branches of the riven pines,
Blurred the white rockets that from dusk till morn
Traced the wide curve of the close-grappling lines.

In rain, and fog that on the withered hill
Froze before dawn, the lurking foe drew down;
Or light snows fell that made forlorner still
The ravaged country and the ruined town;

Or the long clouds would end. Intensely fair,
The winter constellations blazing forth –
Perseus, the Twins, Orion, the Great Bear –
Gleamed on our bayonets pointing to the north.

And the lone sentinel would start and soar
On wings of strong emotion as he knew
That kinship with the stars that only War
Is great enough to lift man's spirit to.

And ever down the curving front, aglow
With the pale rockets' intermittent light,
He heard, like distant thunder, growl and grow
The rumble of far battles in the night, —

Rumors, reverberant, indistinct, remote,
Borne from red fields whose martial names have won
The power to thrill like a far trumpet-note, —
Vic, Vailly, Soupir, Hurtelise, Craonne . . .

Craonne, before thy cannon-swept plateau,
Where like sere leaves lay strewn September's dead,
I found for all dear things I forfeited
A recompense I would not now forego.

For that high fellowship was ours then
With those who, championing another's good,
More than dull Peace or its poor votaries could,
Taught us the dignity of being men.

There we drained deeper the deep cup of life,
And on sublimer summits came to learn,
After soft things, the terrible and stern,
After sweet Love, the majesty of Strife;

There where we faced under those frowning heights
The blast that maims, the hurricane that kills;
There where the watchlights on the winter hills
Flickered like balefire through inclement nights;

There where, firm links in the unyielding chain,
Where fell the long-planned blow and fell in vain –
Hearts worthy of the honor and the trial,
We helped to hold the lines along the Aisne.

Alan Seeger

Champagne, 1914–15

In the glad revels, in the happy fêtes,
When cheeks are flushed, and glasses gilt and pearled
With the sweet wine of France that concentrates
The sunshine and the beauty of the world,

Drink sometimes, you whose footsteps yet may tread
The undisturbed, delightful paths of Earth,
To those whose blood, in pious duty shed,
Hallows the soil where that same wine had birth.

Here, by devoted comrades laid away,
Along our lines they slumber where they fell,
Beside the crater at the Ferme d'Alger
And up the bloody slopes of La Pompelle,

And round the city whose cathedral towers
The enemies of Beauty dared profane,
And in the mat of multicolored flowers
That clothe the sunny chalk-fields of Champagne.

Under the little crosses where they rise
The soldier rests. Now round him undismayed
The cannon thunders, and at night he lies
At peace beneath the eternal fusillade . . .

That other generations might possess –
From shame and menace free in years to come –
A richer heritage of happiness,
He marched to that heroic martyrdom.

Esteeming less the forfeit that he paid
Than undishonored that his flag might float
Over the towers of liberty, he made
His breast the bulwark and his blood the moat.

Obscurely sacrificed, his nameless tomb,
Bare of the sculptor's art, the poet's lines,
Summer shall flush with poppy-fields in bloom,
And Autumn yellow with maturing vines.

There the grape-pickers at their harvesting
Shall lightly tread and load their wicker trays,
Blessing his memory as they toil and sing
In the slant sunshine of October days . . .

I love to think that if my blood should be
So privileged to sink where his has sunk,
I shall not pass from Earth entirely,
But when the banquet rings, when healths are drunk,

And faces that the joys of living fill
Glow radiant with laughter and good cheer,
In beaming cups some spark of me shall still
Brim toward the lips that once I held so dear.

So shall one coveting no higher plane
Than nature clothes in color and flesh and tone,
Even from the grave put upward to attain
The dreams youth cherished and missed and might have
    known;

And that strong need that strove unsatisfied
Toward earthly beauty in all forms it wore,

Not death itself shall utterly divide
From the belovèd shapes it thirsted for.

Alas, how many an adept for whose arms
Life held delicious offerings perished here,
How many in the prime of all that charms,
Crowned with all gifts that conquer and endear!

Honor them not so much with tears and flowers,
But you with whom the sweet fulfilment lies,
Where in the anguish of atrocious hours
Turned their last thoughts and closed their dying eyes,

Rather when music on bright gatherings lays
Its tender spell, and joy is uppermost,
Be mindful of the men they were, and raise
Your glasses to them in one silent toast.

Drink to them – amorous of dear Earth as well,
They asked no tribute lovelier than this –
And in the wine that ripened where they fell,
Oh, frame your lips as though it were a kiss.

Alan Seeger

I Have a Rendezvous with Death

I have a rendezvous with Death
At some disputed barricade,
When Spring comes back with rustling shade
And apple-blossoms fill the air —
I have a rendezvous with Death
When Spring brings back blue days and fair.

It may be he shall take my hand
And lead me into his dark land
And close my eyes and quench my breath —
It may be I shall pass him still.
I have a rendezvous with Death
On some scarred slope of battered hill,
When Spring comes round again this year
And the first meadow-flowers appear.

God knows 'twere better to be deep
Pillowed in silk and scented down,
Where love throbs out in blissful sleep,
Pulse nigh to pulse, and breath to breath,
Where hushed awakenings are dear . . .
But I've a rendezvous with Death
At midnight in some flaming town,
When Spring trips north again this year,
And I to my pledged word am true,
I shall not fail that rendezvous.

Alan Seeger

War

To end the dreary day,
The sun brought fire
And smote the grey
Of the heavens away
In his desire
That the evening sky might glow as red
As showed the earth with blood and ire.

The distant cannon's boom
In a land oppressed
Still spake the gloom
Of a country's doom,
Denying rest.
'War!' – called the frightened rooks and flew
From the crimson East to the crimson West.

Then, lest the dark might mar
The sky o'erhead,
There shone a star,
In the night afar
O'er each man's bed,
A symbol of undying peace,
The peace encompassing the dead.

Richard Dennys

Better Far to Pass Away

Better far to pass away
While the limbs are strong and young,
Ere the ending of the day,
Ere youth's lusty song be sung.
Hot blood pulsing through the veins,
Youth's high hope a burning fire,
Young men needs must break the chains
That hold them from their hearts' desire.

My friends the hills, the sea, the sun,
The winds, the woods, the clouds, the trees –
How feebly, if my youth were done,
Could I, an old man, relish these!
With laughter, then, I'll go to greet
What Fate has still in store for me,
And welcome Death if we should meet,
And bear him willing company.

My share of fourscore years and ten
I'll gladly yield to any man,
And take no thought of 'where' or 'when,'
Contented with my shorter span,
For I have learned what love may be,
And found a heart that understands,
And known a comrade's constancy,
And felt the grip of friendly hands.

Come when it may, the stern decree
For me to leave the cheery throng
And quit the sturdy company
Of brothers that I work among.

No need for me to look askance,
Since no regret my prospect mars.
My day was happy – and perchance
The coming night is full of stars.

Richard Dennys

The Song of Sheffield

Shells, shells, shells!
The song of the city of steel;
Hammer and turn, and file,
Furnace, and lathe, and wheel.
Tireless machinery,
Man's ingenuity,
Making a way for the martial devil's meal.

Shells, shells, shells!
Out of the furnace blaze;
Roll, roll, roll,
Into the workshop's maze.
Ruthless machinery
Boring eternally,
Boring a hole for the shattering charge that stays.

Shells, shells, shells!
The song of the city of steel;
List to the devils' mirth,
Hark to their laughters' peal:
Sheffield's machinery
Crushing humanity
Neath devil-ridden death's impassive heel.

Harold Beckh

To My Daughter Betty, the Gift of God

In wiser days, my darling rosebud, blown
To beauty proud as was your mother's prime,
In that desired, delayed, incredible time,
You'll ask why I abandoned you, my own,
And the dear heart that was your baby throne,
To dice with death. And oh! they'll give you rhyme
And reason: some will call the thing sublime,
And some decry it in a knowing tone.
So here, while the mad guns curse overhead,
And tired men sigh with mud for couch and floor,
Know that we fools, now with the foolish dead,
Died not for flag, nor King, nor Emperor, –
But for a dream, born in a herdsman's shed,
And for the secret Scripture of the poor.

T.M. Kettle

Light After Darkness

Once more the Night, like some great dark drop-scene
Eclipsing horrors for a brief *entr'acte*,
Descends, lead-weighty. Now the space between,
Fringed with the eager eyes of men, is racked
By spark-tailed lights, curvetting far and high,
Swift smoke-flecked coursers, raking the black sky.

And as each sinks in ashes grey, one more
Rises to fall, and so through all the hours
They strive like petty empires by the score,
Each confident of its success and powers,
And, hovering at its zenith, each will show
Pale, rigid faces, lying dead, below.
There shall they lie, tainting the innocent air,
Until the dawn, deep veiled in mournful grey,
Sadly and quietly shall lay them bare,
The broken heralds of a doleful day.

E. Wyndham Tennant

Home Thoughts from Laventie

Green gardens in Laventie!
Soldiers only know the street
Where the mud is churned and splashed about
By battle-wending feet;
And yet beside one stricken house there is a
  glimpse of grass, –
Look for it when you pass.

Beyond the church whose pitted spire
Seems balanced on a strand
Of swaying stone and tottering brick,
Two roofless ruins stand;
And here, among the wreckage, where the back-wall
  should have been,
We found a garden green.

The grass was never trodden on,
The little path of gravel
Was overgrown with celandine;
No other folk did travel
Along its weedy surface but the nimble-footed mouse,
Running from house to house.

So all along the tender blades
Of soft and vivid grass
We lay, nor heard the limber wheels
That pass and ever pass
In noisy continuity until their stony rattle
Seems in itself a battle.

At length we rose up from this ease
Of tranquil happy mind,
And searched the garden's little length
Some new pleasaunce to find;
And there some yellow daffodils, and jasmine
  hanging high,
Did rest the tired eye.

The fairest and most fragrant
Of the many sweets we found
Was a little bush of Daphne flower
Upon a mossy mound,
And so thick were the blossoms set and so divine
  the scent,
That we were well content.

Hungry for Spring I bent my head,
The perfume fanned my face,
And all my soul was dancing
In that lovely little place,
Dancing with a measured step from wrecked and
  shattered towns
Away . . . upon the Downs.

I saw green banks of daffodil,
Slim poplars in the breeze,
Great tan-brown hares in gusty March
A-courting on the leas.
And meadows, with their glittering streams – and
  silver-scurrying dace –
Home, what a perfect place!

E. Wyndham Tennant

The Mad Soldier

I dropp'd here three weeks ago, yes – I know,
And it's bitter cold at night, since the fight –
I could tell you if I chose – no one knows
Excep' me and four or five, what ain't alive
I can see them all asleep, three men deep,
And they're nowhere near a fire – but our wire
Has 'em fast as fast can be. Can't you see
When the flare goes up? Ssh! boys; what's that noise?
Do you know what these rats eat? Body-meat!
After you've been down a week, an' your cheek
Gets as pale as life, and night seems as white
As the day, only the rats and their brats
Seem more hungry when the day's gone away –
An' they look as big as bulls, an' they pulls
Till you almost sort o' shout – but the drought
What you hadn't felt before makes you sore.
And at times you even think of a drink . . .
There's a leg across my thighs – if my eyes
Weren't too sore, I'd like to see who it be,
Wonder if I'd know the bloke if I woke? –
Woke? By damn, I'm not asleep – there's a heap
Of us wond'ring why the hell we're not well . . .
Leastways I am – since I came it's the same
With the others – they don't know what I do,
Or they wouldn't gape and grin. – It's a sin
To say that Hell is hot – 'cause it's not:
Mind you, I know very well we're in hell. –

In a twisted hump we lie – heaping high
Yes! an' higher every day. – Oh, I say,
This chap's heavy on my thighs – damn his eyes.

E. Wyndham Tennant

Reincarnation

I too remember distant golden days
When even my soul was young; I see the sand
Whirl in a blinding pillar towards the band
Of orange sky-line 'neath a turquoise blaze –
(Some burnt-out sky spread o'er a glistening land)
– And slim brown jargoning men in blue and gold,
I know it all so well, I understand
The ecstasy of worship ages-old.

Hear the first truth: The great far-seeing soul
Is ever in the humblest husk; I see
How each succeeding section takes its toll
In fading cycles of old memory.
And each new life the next life shall control
Until perfection reach eternity.

E. Wyndham Tennant

From an Outpost

I've tramped South England up and down
Down Dorset way, down Devon way,
Through every little ancient town
Down Dorset way, down Devon way.
I mind the old stone churches there,
The taverns round the market square,
The cobbled streets, the garden flowers,
The sundials telling peaceful hours
Down Dorset way, down Devon way.

The Meadowlands are green and fair
Down Somerset and Sussex way,
The clover scent is in the air
Down Somerset and Sussex way.
I mind the deep-thatched homesteads there
The noble downlands, clean and bare.
The sheepfolds and the cattle byres,
The blue wood-smoke from shepherds' fires
Down Dorset way, down Devon way.

Mayhap I shall not walk again
Down Dorset way, down Devon way,
Nor pick a posy in a lane
Down Somerset and Sussex way.
But though my bones, unshriven, rot
In some far distant alien spot,

What soul I have shall rest from care
To know that meadows still are fair
Down Dorset way, down Devon way.

Leslie Coulson

The Rainbow

I watch the white dawn gleam,
To the thunder of hidden guns.
I hear the hot shells scream
Through skies as sweet as a dream
Where the silver dawn-break runs.
And stabbing of light
Scorches the virginal white.
But I feel in my being the old, high, sanctified thrill,
And I thank the gods that dawn is beautiful still.

From death that hurtles by
I crouch in the trench day-long
But up to a cloudless sky
From the ground where our dead men lie
A brown lark soars in song.
Through the tortured air,
Rent by the shrapnel's flare,
Over the troubleless dead he carols his fill,
And I thank the gods that the birds are beautiful still.

Where the parapet is low
And level with the eye
Poppies and cornflowers glow
And the corn sways to and fro
In a pattern against the sky.
The gold stalks hide
Bodies of men who died
Charging at dawn through the dew to be killed
  or to kill.
I thank the gods that the flowers are beautiful still.

When night falls dark we creep
In silence to our dead.
We dig a few feet deep
And leave them there to sleep –
But blood at night is red,
Yea, even at night,
And a dead man's face is white.
And I dry my hands, that are also trained to kill,
And I look at the stars – for the stars are beautiful still.

Leslie Coulson

'—But a Short Time to Live'

Our little hour – how swift it flies
When poppies flare and lilies smile;
How soon the fleeting minute dies,
Leaving us but a little while
To dream our dreams, to sing our song,
To pick the fruit, to pluck the flower,
The Gods – They do not give us long, –
One little hour.

Our little hour – how short it is
When Love with dew-eyed loveliness
Raises her lips for ours to kiss
And dies within our first caress.
Youth flickers out like wind-blown flame,
Sweets of to-day to-morrow sour,
For Time and Death, relentless, claim
Our little hour.

Our little hour – how short a time
To wage our wars, to fan our hates,
To take our fill of armoured crime,
To troop our banner, storm the gates.
Blood on the sword, our eyes blood-red,
Blind in our puny reign of power,
Do we forget how soon is sped
Our little hour.

Our little hour – how soon it dies;
How short a time to tell our beads,
To chant our feeble Litanies,
To think sweet thoughts, to do good deeds.

The altar lights grow pale and dim,
The bells hang silent in the tower –
So passes with the dying hymn
Our little hour.

Leslie Coulson

Who Made the Law?

Who made the Law that men should die in meadows?
Who spake the word that blood should splash in lanes?
Who gave it forth that gardens should be bone-yards?
Who spread the hills with flesh, and blood, and brains?
Who made the Law?

Who made the Law that Death should stalk the village?
Who spake the word to kill among the sheaves,
Who gave it forth that death should lurk in hedgerows,
Who flung the dead among the fallen leaves?
Who made the Law?

Those who return shall find that peace endures,
Find old things old, and know the things they knew,
Walk in the garden, slumber by the fireside,
Share the peace of dawn, and dream amid the dew –
Those who return.

Those who return shall till the ancient pastures,
Clean-hearted men shall guide the plough-horse reins,
Some shall grow apples and flowers in the valleys,
Some shall go courting in summer down the lanes –
THOSE WHO RETURN.

But who made the Law? the Trees shall whisper to him:
'See, see the blood – the splashes on our bark!'
Walking the meadows, he shall hear bones crackle,
And fleshless mouths shall gibber in silent lanes at dark.
Who made the Law?

Who made the Law? At noon upon the hillside
His ears shall hear a moan, his cheeks shall feel a
  breath,
And all along the valleys, past gardens, croft, and
  homesteads,
He who made the Law,
HE who made the Law,
HE who made the Law shall walk along with Death.
WHO made the Law?

Leslie Coulson

The Night Patrol

Over the top! The wire's thin here, unbarbed
Plain rusty coils, not staked, and low enough:
Full of old tins, though – 'When you're through, all three,
Aim quarter left for fifty yards or so,
Then straight for that new piece of German wire;
See if it's thick, and listen for a while
For sounds of working; don't run any risks;
About an hour; now, over!'
And we placed
Our hands on the topmost sand-bags, leapt, and stood
A second with curved backs, then crept to the wire,
Wormed ourselves tinkling through, glanced back, and
   dropped.
The sodden ground was splashed with shallow pools,
And tufts of crackling cornstalks, two years old,
No man had reaped, and patches of spring grass,
Half-seen, as rose and sank the flares, were strewn
The wrecks of our attack: the bandoliers,
Packs, rifles, bayonets, belts, and haversacks,
Shell fragments, and the huge whole forms of shells
Shot fruitlessly – and everywhere the dead.
Only the dead were always present – present
As a vile sickly smell of rottenness;
The rustling stubble and the early grass,
The slimy pools – the dead men stank through all,
Pungent and sharp; as bodies loomed before,
And as we passed, they stank: then dulled away
To that vague fœtor, all encompassing,
Infecting earth and air. They lay, all clothed,
Each in some new and piteous attitude
That we well marked to guide us back: as he,

Outside our wire, that lay on his back and crossed
His legs Crusader-wise; I smiled at that,
And thought on Elia and his Temple Church.
From him, at quarter left, lay a small corpse,
Down in a hollow, huddled as in a bed,
That one of us put his hand on unawares.
Next was a bunch of half a dozen men
All blown to bits, an archipelago
Of corrupt fragments, vexing to us three,
Who had no light to see by, save the flares.
On such a trail, so lit, for ninety yards
We crawled on belly and elbows, till we saw,
Instead of lumpish dead before our eyes,
The stakes and crosslines of the German wire.
We lay in shelter of the last dead man,
Ourselves as dead, and heard their shovels ring
Turning the earth, then talk and cough at times.
A sentry fired and a machine-gun spat;
They shot a glare above us, when it fell
And spluttered out in the pools of No Man's Land,
We turned and crawled past the remembered dead:
Past him and him, and them and him, until,
For he lay some way apart, we caught the scent
Of the Crusader and slid past his legs,
And through the wire and home, and got our rum.

Arthur Graeme West

God! How I Hate You, You Young Cheerful Men

God! How I hate you, you young cheerful men,
Whose pious poetry blossoms on your graves
As soon as you are in them, nurtured up
By the salt of your corruption, and the tears
Of mothers, local vicars, college deans,
And flanked by prefaces and photographs
From all your minor poet friends – the fools –
Who paint their sentimental elegies
Where sure, no angel treads; and, living, share
The dead's brief immortality.

Oh Christ!
To think that one could spread the ductile wax
Of his fluid youth to Oxford's glowing fires
And take her seal so ill! Hark how one chants –
'Oh happy to have lived these epic days' –
'These epic days'! And he'd been to France,
And seen the trenches, glimpsed the huddled dead
In the periscope, hung in the rusting wire:
Choked by their sickly fœtor, day and night
Blown down his throat: stumbled through ruined hearths,
Proved all that muddy brown monotony,
Where blood's the only coloured thing. Perhaps
Had seen a man killed, a sentry shot at night,
Hunched as he fell, his feet on the firing-step,
His neck against the back slope of the trench,
And the rest doubled up between, his head
Smashed like an egg-shell, and the warm grey brain
Spattered all bloody on the parados:
Had flashed a torch on his face, and known his friend,
Shot, breathing hardly, in ten minutes – gone!

Yet still God's in His heaven, all is right
In the best possible of worlds. The woe,
Even His scaled eyes must see, is partial, only
A seeming woe, we cannot understand.
God loves us, God looks down on this our strife
And smiles in pity, blows a pipe at times
And calls some warriors home. We do not die,
God would not let us, He is too 'intense',
Too 'passionate', a whole day sorrows He
Because a grass-blade dies. How rare life is!
On earth, the love and fellowship of men,
Men sternly banded: banded for what end?
Banded to maim and kill their fellow men –
For even Huns are men. In heaven above
A genial umpire, a good judge of sport,
Won't let us hurt each other! Let's rejoice
God keeps us faithful, pens us still in fold.
Ah, what a faith is ours (almost, it seems,
Large as a mustard-seed) – we trust and trust,
Nothing can shake us! Ah, how good God is
To suffer us to be born just now, when youth
That else would rust, can slake his blade in gore,
Where very God Himself does seem to walk
The bloody fields of Flanders He so loves!

Arthur Graeme West

In Memoriam (Easter, 1915)

The flowers left thick at nightfall in the wood
This Eastertide call into mind the men,
Now far from home, who, with their sweethearts, should
Have gathered them and will do never again.

Edward Thomas

Gone, Gone Again

Gone, gone again,
May, June, July,
And August gone,
Again gone by,

Not memorable
Save that I saw them go,
As past the empty quays
The rivers flow.

And now again,
In the harvest rain,
The Blenheim oranges
Fall grubby from the trees

As when I was young —
And when the lost one was here —
And when the war began
To turn young men to dung.

Look at the old house,
Outmoded, dignified,
Dark and untenanted,
With grass growing instead

Of the footsteps of life,
The friendliness, the strife;
In its beds have lain
Youth, love, age, and pain:

I am something like that;
Only I am not dead,
Still breathing and interested
In the house that is not dark:—

I am something like that:
Not one pane to reflect the sun,
For the schoolboys to throw at —
They have broken every one.

Edward Thomas

Rain

Rain, midnight rain, nothing but the wild rain
On this bleak hut, and solitude, and me
Remembering again that I shall die
And neither hear the rain nor give it thanks
For washing me cleaner than I have been
Since I was born into this solitude.
Blessed are the dead that the rain rains upon:
But here I pray that none whom once I loved
Is dying to-night or lying still awake
Solitary, listening to the rain,
Either in pain or thus in sympathy
Helpless among the living and the dead,
Like a cold water among broken reeds,
Myriads of broken reeds all still and stiff,
Like me who have no love which this wild rain
Has not dissolved except the love of death,
If love it be for what is perfect and
Cannot, the tempest tells me, disappoint.

Edward Thomas

The Cherry Trees

The cherry trees bend over and are shedding,
On the old road where all that passed are dead,
Their petals, strewing the grass as for a wedding
This early May morn when there is none to wed.

Edward Thomas

As the Team's Head-Brass

As the team's head-brass flashed out on the turn
The lovers disappeared into the wood.
I sat among the boughs of the fallen elm
That strewed the angle of the fallow, and
Watched the plough narrowing a yellow square
Of charlock. Every time the horses turned
Instead of treading me down, the ploughman leaned
Upon the handles to say or ask a word,
About the weather, next about the war.
Scraping the share he faced towards the wood,
And screwed along the furrow till the brass flashed
Once more.
The blizzard felled the elm whose crest
I sat in, by a woodpecker's round hole,
The ploughman said, 'When will they take it away?'
'When the war's over.' So the talk began –
One minute and an interval of ten,
A minute more and the same interval.
'Have you been out?' 'No.' 'And don't want to, perhaps?'
'If I could only come back again, I should.
I could spare an arm, I shouldn't want to lose
A leg. If I should lose my head, why, so,
I should want nothing more . . . Have many gone
From here?' 'Yes.' 'Many lost?' 'Yes, a good few.
Only two teams work on the farm this year.
One of my mates is dead. The second day
In France they killed him. It was back in March,
The very night of the blizzard, too. Now if
He had stayed here we should have moved the tree.'
'And I should not have sat here. Everything
Would have been different. For it would have been

Another world.' 'Ay, and a better, though
If we could see all all might seem good.' Then
The lovers came out of the wood again:
The horses started and for the last time
I watched the clods crumble and topple over
After the ploughshare and the stumbling team.

Edward Thomas

This is No Case of Petty Right or Wrong

This is no case of petty right or wrong
That politicians or philosophers
Can judge. I hate not Germans, nor grow hot
With love of Englishmen, to please newspapers.
Beside my hate for one fat patriot
My hatred of the Kaiser is love true: —
A kind of god he is, banging a gong.
But I have not to choose between the two,
Or between justice and injustice. Dinned
With war and argument I read no more
Than in the storm smoking along the wind
Athwart the wood. Two witches' cauldrons roar.
From one the weather shall rise clear and gay;
Out of the other an England beautiful
And like her mother that died yesterday.
Little I know or care if, being dull,
I shall miss something that historians
Can rake out of the ashes when perchance
The phoenix broods serene above their ken.
But with the best and meanest Englishmen
I am one in crying, God save England, lest
We lose what never slaves and cattle blessed.
The ages made her that made us from dust:
She is all we know and live by, and we trust
She is good and must endure, loving her so:
And as we love ourselves we hate her foe.

Edward Thomas

The Answer

O the Tyrant Lord has drawn his sword,
And has flung the scabbard away.
He has said the word that loosed his horde
To ravage, destroy and slay.
'Then where are those who will dare oppose
The blast of my fury's flame?'
But a salty breeze swept across the seas,
And back the clear answer came:
'We have heard the boast of your mighty host,
And slaves will we ne'er become;
Let our deeds declare what our hearts will dare,
We come! We come! We come!'

J.M. Langstaff

A Listening Post

The sun's a red ball in the oak
And all the grass is grey with dew,
Awhile ago a blackbird spoke –
He didn't know the world's askew.

And yonder rifleman and I
Wait here behind the misty trees
To shoot the first man that goes by,
Our rifles ready on our knees.

How could he know that if we fail
The world may lie in chains for years
And England be a bygone tale
And right be wrong, and laughter tears?

Strange that this bird sits there and sings
While we must only sit and plan –
Who are so much the higher things –
The murder of our fellow man . . .

But maybe God will cause to be –
Who brought forth sweetness from the strong –
Out of our discords harmony
Sweeter than that bird's song.

Robert Ernest Vernède

The Shell Hole

In the Shell Hole he lies, this German soldier of a
    year ago;
But he is not as then, accoutred, well, and eager for
    the foe
He hoped so soon, so utterly, to crush. His muddy
    skull
Lies near the mangled remnants of his corpse – war's
    furies thus annul
The pomp and pageantry that were its own. White
    rigid bones
Gape through the nauseous chaos of his clothes; the
    cruel stones
Hold fast the letter he was wont to clasp close to his
    am'rous breast.
Here 'neath the stark, keen stars, where is no peace,
    no joy, nor any rest,
He lies. There, to the right, his boot, gashed by the great
    shell's fiendish whim,
Retains – O horrid spectacle! – the fleshless stump that
    was his limb!
Vile rats and mice, and flies and lice and ghastly things
    that carrion know
Have made a travesty of Death of him who lived a year
    ago.

Hamish Mann

The Soldier

'Tis strange to look on a man that is dead
As he lies in the shell-swept hell
And to think that the poor black battered corpse
Once lived like you and was well.

'Tis stranger far when you come to think
That you may be soon like him . . .
And it's Fear that tugs at your trembling soul,
A Fear that is weird and grim!

Hamish Mann

Tommy's Dwelling

I come from trenches deep in slime,
Soft slime so sweet and yellow,
And rumble down the steps in time
to souse 'some shivering fellow'.

I trickle in and trickle out
Of every nook and corner,
And, rushing like some waterspout,
Make many a rat a mourner.

I gather in from near and far
A thousand brooklets swelling,
And laugh aloud a great 'Ha, ha!'
To flood poor Tommy's dwelling.

Harold Parry

An April Interlude – 1917

April snow agleam in the stubble,
Melting to brown on the new-ploughed fields,
April sunshine, and swift cloud-shadows
Racing to spy what the season yields
Over the hills and far away:
Heigh! And ho! For an April day!
Hoofs on the highroad: *Ride—tr-r—ot!*
Spring's in the wind, and war's forgot,
As we go riding through Picardy.

Up by a wood where a brown hawk hovers,
Down through a village with white-washed walls,
A wooden bridge and a mill-wheel turning,
And a little stream that sports and brawls
Into the valley and far away:
Heigh! and ho! For an April day!
Children and old men stop to stare
At the chattering horsemen from Angleterre,
As we go riding through Picardy.

On by the unkempt hedges, budding,
On by the Chateau gates flung wide.
Where is the man who should trim the garden?
Where are the youths of this country-side? –
Over the hills and far away
Is war, red war, this April day.
So for the moment we pay our debt
To the cause on which our faith is set,
As we go riding through Picardy.

Then the hiss of the spurted gravel,
Then the tang of wind on the face,
Then the splash of the hoof-deep puddle,
Spirit of April setting the pace
Over the hills and far away:
Heigh! And ho! For an April day!
Heigh! For a ringing: Ride—tr-r—ot!
Ho! – of war we've never a thought
As we go riding through Picardy.

Bernard Freeman Trotter

A Kiss

She kissed me when she said good-bye –
A child's kiss, neither bold nor shy.

We had met but a few short summer hours;
Talked of the sun, the wind, the flowers,

Sports and people; had rambled through
A casual catchy song or two,

And walked with arms linked to the car
By the light of a single misty star.

(It was war-time, you see, and the streets were dark
Lest the ravishing Hun should find a mark.)

And so we turned to say good-bye;
But somehow or other, I don't know why,

– Perhaps 'twas the feel of the khaki coat
(She'd a brother in Flanders then) that smote

Her heart with a sudden tenderness
Which issued in that swift caress –

Somehow, to her, at any rate
A mere hand-clasp seemed inadequate;

And so she lifted her dewy face
And kissed me – but without a trace

Of passion, – and we said good-bye . . .

A child's kiss, . . . neither bold nor shy.

My friend, I like you – it seemed to say –
Here's to our meeting again some day!
Some happier day . . .
Good-bye.

Bernard Freeman Trotter

'Ici Repose'

A little cross of weather-silvered wood,
Hung with a garish wreath of tinselled wire,
And on it carved a legend – thus it runs:
'Ici Repose—' Add what name you will
And multiply by thousands: in the fields,
Along the roads, beneath the trees – one here,
A dozen there, to each its simple tale
Of one more jewel threaded star-like on
The sacrificial rosary of France.

And as I read and read again those words,
Those simple words, they took a mystic sense;
And from the glamour of an alien tongue
They wove insistent music in my brain,
Which, in a twilight hour, when all the guns
Were silent, shaped itself to song.

O happy dead! Who sleep embalmed in glory,
Safe from corruption, purified by fire, –
Ask you our pity? – ours, mud-grimed and gory,
Who still must grimly strive, grimly desire?

You have outrun the reach of our endeavour,
Have flown beyond our most exalted quest, –
Who prate of Faith and Freedom, knowing ever
That all we really fight for's just – a rest,

The rest that only Victory can bring us –
Or Death, which throws us brother-like by you –
The civil commonplace in which 'twill fling us
To neutralize our then too martial hue.

But you have rest from every tribulation
Even in the midst of war; you sleep serene,
Pinnacled on the sorrow of a nation,
In cerements of sacrificial sheen.

Oblivion cannot claim you: our heroic
War-lustred moment, as our youth, will pass
To swell the dusty hoard of Time the Stoic,
That gathers cobwebs in the nether glass.

We shall grow old, and tainted with the rotten
Effluvia of the peace we fought to win,
The bright deeds of our youth will be forgotten,
Effaced by later failure, sloth, or sin;

But you have conquered Time, and sleep forever,
Like gods, with a white halo on your brows —
Your souls our lode-stars, your death-crowned endeavour
That spur that holds the nations to their vows.

Bernard Freeman Trotter

Evening Clouds

A little flock of clouds go down to rest
In some blue corner off the moon's highway,
With shepherd winds that shook them in the West
To borrowed shapes of earth, in bright array,
Perhaps to weave a rainbow's gay festoons
Around the lonesome isle which Brooke has made
A little England full of lovely noons,
Or dot it with his country's mountain shade.

Ah, little wanderers, when you reach that isle
Tell him, with dripping dew, they have not failed,
What he loved most; for late I roamed a while
Thro' English fields and down her rivers sailed;
And they remember him with beauty caught
From old desires of Oriental Spring
Heard in his heart with singing overwrought;
And still on Purley Common gooseboys sing.

Francis Ledwidge

The Dead Kings

All the dead kings came to me
At Rosnaree, where I was dreaming,
A few stars glimmered through the morn,
And down the thorn the dews were streaming.

And every dead king had a story
Of ancient glory, sweetly told.
It was too early for the lark,
But the starry dark had tints of gold.

I listened to the sorrows three
Of that Eire passed into song.
A cock crowed near a hazel croft,
And up aloft dim larks winged strong.

And I, too, told the kings a story
Of later glory, her fourth sorrow:
There was a sound like moving shields
In high green fields and the lowland furrow.

And one said: 'We who yet are kings
Have heard these things lamenting inly.'
Sweet music flowed from many a bill
And on the hill the morn stood queenly.

And one said: 'Over is the singing,
And bell bough ringing, whence we come;
With heavy hearts we'll tread the shadows,
In honey meadows birds are dumb.'

And one said: 'Since the poets perished
And all they cherished in the way,
Their thoughts unsung, like petal showers
Inflame the hours of blue and grey.'

And one said: 'A loud tramp of men
We'll hear again at Rosnaree.'
A bomb burst near me where I lay.
I woke, 'twas day in Picardy.

Francis Ledwidge

To One Dead

A blackbird singing
On a moss-upholstered stone,
Bluebells swinging,
Shadows wildly blown,
A song in the wood,
A ship on the sea.
The song was for you
And the ship was for me.

A blackbird singing
I hear in my troubled mind,
Bluebells swinging
I see in a distant wind.
But sorrow and silence
Are the wood's threnody,
The silence for you
And the sorrow for me.

Francis Ledwidge

The Place

Blossoms as old as May I scatter here,
And a blue wave I lifted from the stream.
It shall not know when winter days are drear
Or March is hoarse with blowing. But a-dream
The laurel boughs shall hold a canopy
Peacefully over it the winter long,
Till all the birds are back from oversea,
And April rainbows win a blackbird's song.

And when the war is over I shall take
My lute a-down to it and sing again
Songs of the whispering things amongst the brake,
And those I love shall know them by their strain.
Their airs shall be the blackbird's song,
Their words shall be all flowers with fresh dews hoar. –
But it is lonely now in winter long,
And, God! to hear the blackbird song once more.

Francis Ledwidge

The Unconquered Dead

'. . . defeated, with great loss.'

Not we the conquered! Not to us the blame
Of them that flee, of them that basely yield;
Nor ours the shout of victory, the fame
Of them that vanquish in a stricken field.

That day of battle in the dusty heat
We lay and heard the bullets swish and sing
Like scythes amid the over-ripened wheat,
And we the harvest of their garnering.

Some yielded, No, not we! Not we, we swear
By these our wounds; this trench upon the hill
Where all the shell-strewn earth is seamed and bare,
Was ours to keep; and lo! we have it still.

We might have yielded, even we, but death
Came for our helper; like a sudden flood
The crashing darkness fell; our painful breath
We drew with gasps amid the choking blood.

The roar fell faint and farther off, and soon
Sank to a foolish humming in our ears,
Like crickets in the long, hot afternoon
Among the wheat fields of the olden years.

Before our eyes a boundless wall of red
Shot through by sudden streaks of jagged pain!
Then a slow-gathering darkness overhead
And rest came on us like a quiet rain.

Not we the conquered! Not to us the shame,
Who hold our earthen ramparts, nor shall cease
To hold them ever; victors we, who came
In that fierce moment to our honoured peace.

John McCrae

In Flanders Fields

In Flanders fields the poppies blow
Between the crosses, row on row,
That mark our place; and in the sky
The larks, still bravely singing, fly
Scarce heard amid the guns below.

We are the Dead. Short days ago
We lived, felt dawn, saw sunset glow,
Loved and were loved, and now we lie
In Flanders fields.

Take up our quarrel with the foe:
To you from failing hands we throw
The torch; be yours to hold it high.
If ye break faith with us who die
We shall not sleep, though poppies grow
In Flanders fields.

John McCrae

The Anxious Dead

O guns, fall silent till the dead men hear
Above their heads the legions pressing on:
(These fought their fight in time of bitter fear,
And died not knowing how the day had gone.)

O flashing muzzles, pause, and let them see
The coming dawn that streaks the sky afar;
Then let your mighty chorus witness be
To them, and Caesar, that we still make war.

Tell them, O guns, that we have heard their call,
That we have sworn, and will not turn aside,
That we will onward till we win or fall,
That we will keep the faith for which they died.

Bid them be patient, and some day, anon,
They shall feel earth enwrapt in silence deep;
Shall greet, in wonderment, the quiet dawn,
And in content may turn them to their sleep.

John McCrae

The Kitchener Chap

He wore twin stripes of gold upon
An empty tunic sleeve;
His eyes were blue, his face so young
One hardly could believe
That he had seen the death and hate
That make the whole world grieve.

His hair was fair, his eyes were blue,
I thought that I could see
(Just when his sunny smile came through)
The lad he used to be:
Dear happy little mother's lad
Of only two or three.

But when across his eyes there came
A sudden look of pain –
His mouth set very hard and straight,
He was a man again.
He gave his shattered dreams of youth
That England might remain.

I felt hot tears rise to my eyes
When I looked at the lad;
Brave, gallant, shattered, smiling youth –
He gave us all he had;
For youth so fair, so sorely hurt
All England's heart is sad.

He passed me on a crowded street,
We did not meet again;
He showed me in a sudden flash

Our England's pride and pain.
And when all is long forgot
His memory shall remain.

Horace Bray

Marching

(As Seen from the Left File)

My eyes catch ruddy necks
Sturdily pressed back –
All a red brick moving glint.
Like flaming pendulums, hands
Swing across the khaki –
Mustard-coloured khaki –
To the automatic feet.

We husband the ancient glory
In these bared necks and hands.
Not broke is the forge of Mars;
But a subtler brain beats iron
To shoe the hoofs of death
(Who paws dynamic air now).
Blind fingers loose an iron cloud
To rain immortal darkness
On strong eyes.

Isaac Rosenberg

Dead Man's Dump

The plunging limbers over the shattered track
Racketed with their rusty freight,
Stuck out like many crowns of thorns,
And the rusty stakes like sceptres old
To stay the flood of brutish men
Upon our brothers dear.

The wheels lurched over sprawled dead
But pained them not, though their bones crunched,
Their shut mouths made no moan.
They lie there huddled, friend and foeman,
Man born of man, and born of woman,
And shells go crying over them
From night till night and now.

Earth has waited for them,
All the time of their growth
Fretting for their decay:
Now she has them at last!
In the strength of their strength
Suspended – stopped and held.

What fierce imaginings their dark souls lit?
Earth! have they gone into you?
Somewhere they must have gone,
And flung on your hard back
Is their souls' sack,
Emptied of God-ancestralled essences.
Who hurled them out? Who hurled?

None saw their spirits' shadow shake the grass,
Or stood aside for the half-used life to pass
Out of those doomed nostrils and the doomed mouth,
When the swift iron burning bee
Drained the wild honey of their youth.
What of us who, flung on the shrieking pyre,
Walk, our usual thoughts untouched,
Our lucky limbs as on ichor fed,
Immortal seeming ever?
Perhaps when the flames beat loud on us,
A fear may choke in our veins
And the startled blood may stop.

The air is loud with death,
The dark air spurts with fire
The explosions ceaseless are.
Timelessly now, some minutes past,
These dead strode time with vigorous life,
Till the shrapnel called 'An end!'
But not to all. In bleeding pangs
Some borne on stretchers dreamed of home,
Dear things, war-blotted from their hearts.

A man's brains splattered on
A stretcher-bearer's face;
His shook shoulders slipped their load,
But when they bent to look again
The drowning soul was sunk too deep
For human tenderness.

They left this dead with the older dead,
Stretched at the cross roads.

Burnt black by strange decay,
Their sinister faces lie;
The lid over each eye,
The grass and coloured clay
More motions have then they,
Joined to the great sunk silences.

Here is one not long dead;
His dark hearing caught our far wheels,
And the choked soul stretched weak hands
To reach the living word the far wheels said,
The blood-dazed intelligence beating for light,
Crying through the suspense of the far torturing wheels
Swift for the end to break,
Or the wheels to break,
Cried as the tide of the world broke over his sight,
'Will they come? Will they ever come?'
Even as the mixed hoofs of the mules,
The quivering-bellied mules,
And the rushing wheels all mixed
With his tortured upturned sight,

So we crashed round the bend,
We heard his weak scream,
We heard his very last sound,
And our wheels grazed his dead face.

Isaac Rosenberg

On Receiving News of the War

Snow is a strange white word;
No ice or frost
Have asked of bud or bird
For Winter's cost.

Yet ice and frost and snow
From earth to sky
This Summer land doth know.
No man knows why.

In all men's hearts it is.
Some spirit old
Hath turned with malign kiss
Our lives to mould.

Red fangs have torn His face.
God's blood is shed.
He mourns from His lone place
His children dead.

O! ancient crimson curse!
Corrode, consume.
Give back this universe
Its pristine bloom.

Isaac Rosenberg

Louse Hunting

Nudes – stark and glistening,
Yelling in lurid glee. Grinning faces
And raging limbs
Whirl over the floor one fire.
For a shirt verminously busy
Yon soldier tore from his throat, with oaths
Godhead might shrink at, but not the lice.
And soon the shirt was aflare
Over the candle he'd lit while we lay.

Then we all sprang up and stript
To hunt the verminous brood.
Soon like a demons' pantomime
The place was raging.
See the silhouettes agape,
See the glibbering shadows
Mixed with the battled arms on the wall.
See gargantuan hooked fingers
Pluck in supreme flesh
To smutch supreme littleness.
See the merry limbs in hot Highland fling
Because some wizard vermin
Charmed from the quiet this revel
When our ears were half lulled
By the dark music
Blown from Sleep's trumpet.

Isaac Rosenberg

Break of Day in the Trenches

The darkness crumbles away.
It is the same old druid Time as ever,
Only a live thing leaps my hand,
A queer sardonic rat,
As I pull the parapet's poppy
To stick behind my ear.
Droll rat, they would shoot you if they knew
Your cosmopolitan sympathies.
Now you have touched this English hand
You will do the same to a German
Soon, no doubt, if it be your pleasure
To cross the sleeping green between.
It seems you inwardly grin as you pass
Strong eyes, fine limbs, haughty athletes,
Less chanced than you for life,
Bonds to the whims of murder,
Sprawled in the bowels of the earth,
The torn fields of France.
What do you see in our eyes
At the shrieking iron and flame
Hurled through still heavens?
What quaver – what heart aghast?
Poppies whose roots are in man's veins
Drop, and are ever dropping;
But mine in my ear is safe –
Just a little white with the dust.

Isaac Rosenberg

Returning, We Hear the Larks

Sombre the night is.
And though we have our lives, we know
What sinister threat lurks there.

Dragging these anguished limbs, we only know
This poison-blasted track opens on our camp –
On a little safe sleep.

But hark! joy – joy – strange joy.
Lo! heights of night ringing with unseen larks.
Music showering on our upturned list'ning faces.

Death could drop from the dark
As easily as song –
But song only dropped,
Like a blind man's dreams on the sand
By dangerous tides,
Like a girl's dark hair for she dreams no ruin lies there,
Or her kisses where a serpent hides.

Isaac Rosenberg

Casualty List

How long, how long
shall there be Something
that can grind the faces of poor men
to an ultimate uniformity of dullness
and grinning trivial meanness?

Or pitchfork them at will
(cheering and singing patriotic doggerel)
to a stinking hell,
noisily, miserably;
till the inevitable comes,
and crushes them
bloodily, meanly?

Henry Lamont Simpson

Last Song

All my songs are risen and fled away;
(Only the brave birds stay);
All my beautiful songs are broken or fled.
My poor songs could not stay
Among the filth and the weariness and the dead.

There was bloody grime on their light, white feathery
  wings,
(Hear how the lark still sings),
And their eyes were the eyes of dead men that I knew.
Only a madman sings
When half of his friends lie asleep for the rain and the
  dew.

The flowers will grow over the bones of my friends;
(The birds' song never ends);
Winter and summer, their fair flesh turns to clay.
Perhaps before all ends
My songs will come again that have fled away.

Henry Lamont Simpson

Rouge Bouquet

In a wood they call the Rouge Bouquet
There is a new-made grave to-day,
Built by never a spade nor pick
Yet covered with earth ten metres thick.
There lie many fighting men,
Dead in their youthful prime,
Never to laugh nor love again
Nor taste the Summertime.
For Death came flying through the air
And stopped his flight at the dugout stair,
Touched his prey and left them there,
Clay to clay.
He hid their bodies stealthily
In the soil of the land they fought to free
And fled away.
Now over the grave abrupt and clear
Three volleys ring;
And perhaps their brave young spirits hear
The bugle sing:
'Go to sleep
Go to sleep!
Slumber well where the shell screamed and fell.
Let your rifles rest on the muddy floor,
You will not need them any more.
Danger's past;
Now at last,
Go to sleep!'

There is on earth no worthier grave
To hold the bodies of the brave
Than this place of pain and pride

Where they nobly fought and nobly died.
Never fear but in the skies
Saints and angels stand
Smiling with their holy eyes
On this new-come band.
St Michael's sword darts through the air
And touches the aureole on his hair
As he sees them stand saluting there,
His stalwart sons;
And Patrick, Brigid, Columkill
Rejoice that in veins of warriors still
The Gael's blood runs.
And up to Heaven's doorway floats
From the wood called Rouge Bouquet,
A delicate cloud of bugle notes
That softly say:
'Farewell!
Farewell!
Comrades true, born anew, peace to you!
Your souls shall be where the heroes are
And your memory shine like the morning-star.
Brave and dear,
Shield us here.
Farewell!'

Joyce Kilmer

Spring Offensive

Halted against the shade of a last hill,
They fed, and lying easy, were at ease
And, finding comfortable chest and knees
Carelessly slept. But many there stood still
To face the stark, blank sky beyond the ridge,
Knowing their feet had come to the end of the world.

Marvelling they stood, and watched the long grass swirled
By the May breeze, murmurous with wasp and midge,
For though the summer oozed into their veins
Like the injected drug for their bodies' pains,
Sharp on their souls hung the imminent line of grass,
Fearfully flashed the sky's mysterious glass.

Hour after hour they ponder in the warm field, –
And the far valley behind, where the buttercups
Had blessed with gold their slow boots coming up,
When even the little brambles would not yield
But clutched and clung to them like sorrowing hands.
They breathe like trees unstirred.

Till like a cold gust thrilled the little word
At which each body and its soul begird
And tighten them for battle. No alarms
Of bugles, no high flags, no clamorous haste, –
Only a lift and flare of eyes that faced
The sun, like a friend with whom their love is done.
O larger shone that smile against the sun, –
Mightier than his whose bounty these have spurned.

So, soon they topped the hill, and raced together
Over an open stretch of herb and heather
Exposed. And instantly the whole sky burned
With fury against them; earth set sudden cups
In thousands for their blood; and the green slope
Chasmed and steepened sheer to infinite space.

Of them who running on that last high place
Leapt to swift unseen bullets, or went up
On the hot blast and fury of hell's upsurge,
Or plunged and fell away past this world's verge,
Some say God caught them even before they fell.

But what say such as from existence' brink
Ventured but drave too swift to sink,
The few who rushed in the body to enter hell,
And there out-fiending all its fiends and flames
With superhuman inhumanities,
Long-famous glories, immemorial shames –
And crawling slowly back, have by degrees
Regained cool peaceful air in wonder –
Why speak not they of comrades that went under?

Wilfred Owen

Mental Cases

Who are these? Why sit they here in twilight?
Wherefore rock they, purgatorial shadows,
Drooping tongues from jaws that slob their relish,
Baring teeth that leer like skulls' teeth wicked?
Stroke on stroke of pain, – but what slow panic,
Gouged these chasms round their fretted sockets?
Ever from their hair and through their hands' palms
Misery swelters. Surely we have perished
Sleeping, and walk hell; but who these hellish?

—These are men whose minds the Dead have ravished.
Memory fingers in their hair of murders,
Multitudinous murders they once witnessed.
Wading sloughs of flesh these helpless wander,
Treading blood from lungs that had loved laughter.
Always they must see these things and hear them,
Batter of guns and shatter of flying muscles,
Carnage incomparable, and human squander
Rucked too thick for these men's extrication.

Therefore still their eyeballs shrink tormented
Back into their brains, because on their sense
Sunlight seems a bloodsmear; night comes blood-black;
Dawn breaks open like a wound that bleeds afresh.
—Thus their heads wear this hilarious, hideous,
Awful falseness of set-smiling corpses.
—Thus their hands are plucking at each other;

Picking at the rope-knouts of their scourging;
Snatching after us who smote them, brother,
Pawing us who dealt them war and madness.

Wilfred Owen

Disabled

He sat in a wheeled chair, waiting for dark,
And shivered in his ghastly suit of grey,
Legless, sewn short at elbow. Through the park
Voices of boys rang saddening like a hymn,
Voices of play and pleasure after day,
Till gathering sleep had mothered them from him.

About this time Town used to swing so gay
When glow-lamps budded in the light blue trees,
And girls glanced lovelier as the air grew dim,
– In the old times, before he threw away his knees.
Now he will never feel again how slim
Girls' waists are, or how warm their subtle hands.
All of them touch him like some queer disease.

There was an artist silly for his face,
For it was younger than his youth, last year.
Now, he is old; his back will never brace;
He's lost his colour very far from here,
Poured it down shell-holes till the veins ran dry,
And half his lifetime lapsed in the hot race
And leap of purple spurted from his thigh.

One time he liked a bloodsmear down his leg,
After the matches, carried shoulder-high.
It was after football, when he'd drunk a peg,
He thought he'd better join. – He wonders why.
Someone had said he'd look a god in kilts,
That's why; and maybe, too, to please his Meg,
Aye, that was it, to please the giddy jilts
He asked to join. He didn't have to beg;

Smiling they wrote his lie: aged nineteen years.
Germans he scarcely thought of; all their guilt
And Austria's, did not move him. And no fears
Of Fear came yet. He thought of jewelled hilts
For daggers in plaid socks; of smart salutes;
And care of arms; and leave; and pay arrears;
Esprit de corps; and hints for young recruits.
And soon, he was drafted out with drums and cheers.

Some cheered him home, but not as crowds cheer Goal.
Only a solemn man who brought him fruits
Thanked him; and then enquired about his soul.
Now, he will spend a few sick years in institutes,
And do what things the rules consider wise,
And take whatever pity they may dole.
Tonight he noticed how the women's eyes
Passed from him to the strong men that were whole.
How cold and late it is! Why don't they come
And put him into bed? Why don't they come?

Wilfred Owen

Futility

Move him into the sun –
Gently its touch awoke him once,
At home, whispering of fields unsown.
Always it woke him, even in France,
Until this morning and this snow.
If anything might rouse him now
The kind old sun will know.

Think how it wakes the seeds, –
Woke, once, the clays of a cold star.
Are limbs, so dear-achieved, are sides,
Full-nerved, – still warm, – too hard to stir?
Was it for this the clay grew tall?
– O what made fatuous sunbeams toil
To break earth's sleep at all?

Wilfred Owen

Smile, Smile, Smile

Head to limp head, the sunk-eyed wounded scanned
Yesterday's Mail; the casualties (typed small)
And (large) Vast Booty from our Latest Haul.
Also, they read of Cheap Homes, not yet planned,
For, said the paper, when this war is done
The men's first instincts will be making homes.
Meanwhile their foremost need is aerodromes,
It being certain war has but begun.
Peace would do wrong to our undying dead, –
The sons we offered might regret they died
If we got nothing lasting in their stead.
We must be solidly indemnified.
Though all be worthy Victory which all bought,
We rulers sitting in this ancient spot
Would wrong our very selves if we forgot
The greatest glory will be theirs who fought,
Who kept this nation in integrity.
Nation? – The half-limbed readers did not chafe
But smiled at one another curiously
Like secret men who know their secret safe.
(This is the thing they know and never speak,
That England one by one had fled to France,
Not many elsewhere now, save under France.)
Pictures of these broad smiles appear each week,
And people in whose voice real feeling rings
Say: How they smile! They're happy now, poor things.

Wilfred Owen

Anthem for Doomed Youth

What passing-bells for these who die as cattle?
– Only the monstrous anger of the guns.
Only the stuttering rifles' rapid rattle
Can patter out their hasty orisons.
No mockeries now for them; no prayers nor bells;
Nor any voice of mourning save the choirs, –
The shrill, demented choirs of wailing shells;
And bugles calling for them from sad shires.

What candles may be held to speed them all?
Not in the hands of boys, but in their eyes
Shall shine the holy glimmers of goodbyes.
The pallor of girls' brows shall be their pall;
Their flowers the tenderness of patient minds,
And each slow dusk a drawing-down of blinds.

Wilfred Owen

Strange Meeting

It seemed that out of the battle I escaped
Down some profound dull tunnel, long since scooped
Through granites which titanic wars had groined.

Yet also there encumbered sleepers groaned,
Too fast in thought or death to be bestirred.
Then, as I probed them, one sprang up, and stared
With piteous recognition in fixed eyes,
Lifting distressful hands as if to bless.
And by his smile, I knew that sullen hall, –
By his dead smile I knew we stood in Hell.

With a thousand pains that vision's face was grained;
Yet no blood reached there from the upper ground,
And no guns thumped, or down the flues made moan.
'Strange friend,' I said, 'here is no cause to mourn.'
'None,' said the other, 'save the undone years,
The hopelessness. Whatever hope is yours,
Was my life also; I went hunting wild
After the wildest beauty in the world,
Which lies not calm in eyes, or braided hair;
But mocks the steady running of the hour,
And if it grieves, grieves richlier than here.
For by my glee might many men have laughed,
And of my weeping something has been left,
Which must die now. I mean the truth untold,
The pity of war, the pity war distilled.
Now men will go content with what we spoiled,
Or, discontent, boil bloody, and be spilled.
They will be swift with swiftness of the tigress.
None will break ranks, though nations trek from progress.

Courage was mine, and I had mystery,
Wisdom was mine, and I had mastery:
To miss the march of this retreating world
Into vain citadels that are not walled.
Then, when much blood had clogged their chariot-wheels,
I would go up and wash them from sweet wells,
Even with truths that lie too deep for taint.
I would have poured my spirit without stint
But not through wounds; not on the cess of war.
Foreheads of men have bled where no wounds were.

'I am the enemy you killed, my friend.
I knew you in this dark: for so you frowned
Yesterday through me as you jabbed and killed.
I parried; but my hands were loath and cold.
Let us sleep now . . .'

Wilfred Owen

Dulce et Decorum Est

Bent double, like old beggars under sacks,
Knock-kneed, coughing like hags, we cursed through
   sludge,
Till on the haunting flares we turned our backs
And towards our distant rest began to trudge.
Men marched asleep. Many had lost their boots
But limped on, blood-shod. All went lame; all blind;
Drunk with fatigue; deaf even to the hoots
Of tired, outstripped Five-Nines that dropped behind.

Gas! GAS! Quick, boys! – An ecstasy of fumbling,
Fitting the clumsy helmets just in time;
But someone still was yelling out and stumbling,
And flound'ring like a man in fire or lime –
Dim, through the misty panes and thick green light,
As under a green sea, I saw him drowning.
In all my dreams, before my helpless sight,
He plunges at me, guttering, choking, drowning.

If in some smothering dreams you too could pace
Behind the wagon that we flung him in,
And watch the white eyes writhing in his face,
His hanging face, like a devil's sick of sin;
If you could hear, at every jolt, the blood
Come gargling from the froth-corrupted lungs,
Obscene as cancer, bitter as the cud
Of vile, incurable sores on innocent tongues, –
My friend, you would not tell with such high zest

To children ardent for some desperate glory,
The old Lie; *Dulce et Decorum est*
Pro patria mori.

Wilfred Owen

Apologia Pro Poemate Meo

I, too, saw God through mud -
  The mud that cracked on cheeks when wretches smiled.
  War brought more glory to their eyes than blood,
  And gave their laughs more glee than shakes a child.

Merry it was to laugh there –
  Where death becomes absurd and life absurder.
  For power was on us as we slashed bones bare
  Not to feel sickness or remorse of murder.

I, too, have dropped off fear –
  Behind the barrage, dead as my platoon,
  And sailed my spirit surging, light and clear
  Past the entanglement where hopes lay strewn;

And witnessed exultation –
  Faces that used to curse me, scowl for scowl,
  Shine and lift up with passion of oblation,
  Seraphic for an hour; though they were foul.

I have made fellowships –
  Untold of happy lovers in old song.
  For love is not the binding of fair lips
  With the soft silk of eyes that look and long,

By Joy, whose ribbon slips, –
  But wound with war's hard wire whose stakes are strong;
  Bound with the bandage of the arm that drips;
  Knit in the webbing of the rifle-thong.

I have perceived much beauty
   In the hoarse oaths that kept our courage straight;
   Heard music in the silentness of duty;
   Found peace where shell-storms spouted reddest spate.

Nevertheless, except you share
   With them in hell the sorrowful dark of hell,
   Whose world is but the trembling of a flare,
   And heaven but as the highway for a shell,

You shall not hear their mirth:
   You shall not come to think them well content
   By any jest of mine. These men are worth
   Your tears. You are not worth their merriment.

Wilfred Owen

On Being Asked for a War Poem

I think it better that in times like these
A poet's mouth be silent, for in truth
We have no gift to set a statesman right;
He has had enough of meddling who can please
A young girl in the indolence of her youth,
Or an old man upon a winter's night.

William Butler Yeats

An Irish Airman Foresees His Death

I know that I shall meet my fate
Somewhere among the clouds above;
Those that I fight I do not hate,
Those that I guard I do not love;
My country is Kiltartan Cross,
My countrymen Kiltartan's poor,
No likely end could bring them loss
Or leave them happier than before.
Nor law, nor duty bade me fight,
Nor public men, nor cheering crowds,
A lonely impulse of delight
Drove to this tumult in the clouds;
I balanced all, brought all to mind,
The years to come seemed waste of breath,
A waste of breath the years behind
In balance with this life, this death.

William Butler Yeats

Channel Firing

That night your great guns, unawares,
Shook all our coffins as we lay,
And broke the chancel window-squares,
We thought it was the Judgment-day

And sat upright. While drearisome
Arose the howl of wakened hounds:
The mouse let fall the altar-crumb,
The worms drew back into the mounds,

The glebe cow drooled. Till God called, 'No;
It's gunnery practice out at sea
Just as before you went below;
The world is as it used to be:

'All nations striving strong to make
Red war yet redder. Mad as hatters
They do no more for Christés sake
Than you who are helpless in such matters.

'That this is not the judgment-hour
For some of them's a blessed thing,
For if it were they'd have to scour
Hell's floor for so much threatening . . .

'Ha, ha. It will be warmer when
I blow the trumpet (if indeed
I ever do; for you are men,
And rest eternal sorely need).'

So down we lay again. 'I wonder,
Will the world ever saner be,'
Said one, 'than when He sent us under
In our indifferent century!'

And many a skeleton shook his head.
'Instead of preaching forty year,'
My neighbour Parson Thirdly said,
'I wish I had stuck to pipes and beer.'

Again the guns disturbed the hour,
Roaring their readiness to avenge,
As far inland as Stourton Tower,
And Camelot, and starlit Stonehenge.

Thomas Hardy

Men Who March Away

What of the faith and fire within us
Men who march away
Ere the barn-cocks say
Night is growing gray,
Leaving all that here can win us;
What of the faith and fire within us
Men who march away?

Is it a purblind prank, O think you,
Friend with the musing eye,
Who watch us stepping by
With doubt and dolorous sigh?
Can much pondering so hoodwink you!
Is it a purblind prank, O think you,
Friend with the musing eye?

Nay. We well see what we are doing,
Though some may not see –
Dalliers as they be –
England's need are we;
Her distress would leave us rueing:
Nay. We well see what we are doing,
Though some may not see!

In our heart of hearts believing
Victory crowns the just,
And that braggarts must
Surely bite the dust,
Press we to the field ungrieving,
In our heart of hearts believing
Victory crowns the just.

Hence the faith and fire within us
Men who march away
Ere the barn-cocks say
Night is growing gray,
Leaving all that here can win us;
Hence the faith and fire within us
Men who march away.

Thomas Hardy

And There Was a Great Calm

(On the Signing of the Armistice, 11 Nov. 1918)

I

There had been years of Passion – scorching, cold,
And much Despair, and Anger heaving high,
Care whitely watching, Sorrows manifold,
Among the young, among the weak and old,
And the pensive Spirit of Pity whispered, 'Why?'

II

Men had not paused to answer. Foes distraught
Pierced the thinned peoples in a brute-like blindness,
Philosophies that sages long had taught,
And Selflessness, were as an unknown thought,
And 'Hell!' and 'Shell!' were yapped at Lovingkindness.

III

The feeble folk at home had grown full-used
To 'dug-outs', 'snipers', 'Huns', from the war-adept
In the mornings heard, and at evetides perused;
To day-dreamt men in millions, when they mused –
To nightmare-men in millions when they slept.

IV

Waking to wish existence timeless, null,
Sirius they watched above where armies fell;
He seemed to check his flapping when, in the lull
Of night a boom came thencewise, like the dull
Plunge of a stone dropped into some deep well.

V

So, when old hopes that earth was bettering slowly
Were dead and damned, there sounded 'War is done!'
One morrow. Said the bereft, and meek, and lowly,
'Will men some day be given to grace? yea, wholly,
And in good sooth, as our dreams used to run?'

VI

Breathless they paused. Out there men raised their glance
To where had stood those poplars lank and lopped,
As they had raised it through the four years' dance
Of Death in the now familiar flats of France;
And murmured, 'Strange, this! How? All firing stopped?'

VII

Aye; all was hushed. The about-to-fire fired not,
The aimed-at moved away in trance-lipped song.
One checkless regiment slung a clinching shot
And turned. The Spirit of Irony smirked out, 'What?
Spoil peradventures woven of Rage and Wrong?'

VIII

Thenceforth no flying fires inflamed the gray,
No hurtlings shook the dewdrop from the thorn,
No moan perplexed the mute bird on the spray;
Worn horses mused: 'We are not whipped to-day;'
No weft-winged engines blurred the moon's thin horn.

IX

Calm fell. From Heaven distilled a clemency;
There was peace on earth, and silence in the sky;

Some could, some could not, shake off misery:
The Sinister Spirit sneered: 'It had to be!'
And again the Spirit of Pity whispered, 'Why?'

Thomas Hardy

My Boy Jack

'Have you news of my boy Jack?'
Not this tide.
'When d'you think that he'll come back?'
Not with this wind blowing, and this tide.

'Has any one else had word of him?'
Not this tide.
For what is sunk will hardly swim,
Not with this wind blowing, and this tide.

'Oh, dear, what comfort can I find?'
None this tide,
Nor any tide,
Except he did not shame his kind —
Not even with that wind blowing, and that tide.

Then hold your head up all the more,
This tide,
And every tide;
Because he was the son you bore,
And gave to that wind blowing and that tide.

Rudyard Kipling

Epitaphs of the War

'EQUALITY OF SACRIFICE'
A. 'I was a Have.' B. 'I was a "have-not."'
  (*Together*). 'What hast thou given which I gave not?'

A SERVANT
We were together since the War began.
He was my servant — and the better man.

A SON
My son was killed while laughing at some jest. I
  would I knew
What it was, and it might serve me in a time when
  jests are few.

AN ONLY SON
I have slain none except my Mother. She
(Blessing her slayer) died of grief for me.

EX-CLERK
Pity not! The Army gave
Freedom to a timid slave:
In which Freedom did he find
Strength of body, will, and mind:
By which strength he came to prove
Mirth, Companionship, and Love:
For which Love to Death he went:
In which Death he lies content.

THE WONDER
Body and Spirit I surrendered whole

To harsh Instructors – and received a soul . . .
If mortal man could change me through and through
From all I was – what may The God not do?

HINDU SEPOY IN FRANCE
This man in his own country prayed we know not to what
  Powers.
We pray Them to reward him for his bravery in ours.

THE COWARD
I could not look on Death, which being known,
Men led me to him, blindfold and alone.

SHOCK
My name, my speech, my self I had forgot.
My wife and children came – I knew them not.
I died. My Mother followed. At her call
And on her bosom I remembered all.

A GRAVE NEAR CAIRO
Gods of the Nile, should this stout fellow here
Get out – get out!
He knows not shame nor fear.

PELICANS IN THE WILDERNESS
A Grave near Halfa

The blown sand heaps on me, that none may learn
Where I am laid for whom my children grieve . . .
O wings that beat at dawning, ye return
Out of the desert to your young at eve!

TWO CANADIAN MEMORIALS

I

We giving all gained all.
  Neither lament us nor praise.
Only in all things recall,
  It is Fear, not Death that slays.

II

From little towns in a far land we came,
  To save our honour and a world aflame.
By little towns in a far land we sleep;
  And trust that world we won for you to keep!

THE FAVOUR

Death favoured me from the first, well knowing I could
    not endure
To wait on him day by day. He quitted my betters and came
Whistling over the fields, and, when he had made all sure,
'Thy line is at end,' he said, 'but at least I have saved its
    name.'

THE BEGINNER

On the first hour of my first day
In the front trench I fell.
(Children in boxes at a play
Stand up to watch it well.)

R.A.F. (AGED EIGHTEEN)

Laughing through clouds, his milk-teeth still unshed,
Cities and men he smote from overhead.
His deaths delivered, he returned to play
Childlike, with childish things now put away.

THE REFINED MAN

I was of delicate mind. I stepped aside for my needs,
Disdaining the common office. I was seen from afar and
  killed . . .
How is this matter for mirth? Let each man be judged by
  his deeds.
I have paid my price to live with myself on the terms that I willed.

NATIVE WATER-CARRIER (M.E.F.)

Prometheus brought down fire to men,
This brought up water.
The Gods are jealous – now, as then,
Giving no quarter.

BOMBED IN LONDON

On land and sea I strove with anxious care
To escape conscription. It was in the air!

THE SLEEPY SENTINEL

Faithless the watch that I kept: now I have none to keep.
I was slain because I slept: now I am slain I sleep.
Let no man reproach me again, whatever watch is
  unkept—
I sleep because I am slain. They slew me because I slept.

BATTERIES OUT OF AMMUNITION

If any mourn us in the workshop, say
We died because the shift kept holiday.

COMMON FORM

If any question why we died,
Tell them, because our fathers lied.

A DEAD STATESMAN

I could not dig: I dared not rob:
Therefore I lied to please the mob.
Now all my lies are proved untrue
And I must face the men I slew.
What tale shall serve me here among
Mine angry and defrauded young?

THE REBEL

If I had clamoured at Thy Gate
For gift of Life on Earth,
And, thrusting through the souls that wait,
Flung headlong into birth—
Even then, even then, for gin and snare
About my pathway spread,
Lord, I had mocked Thy thoughtful care
Before I joined the Dead!
But now? . . . I was beneath Thy Hand
Ere yet the Planets came.
And now – though Planets pass, I stand
The witness to Thy shame!

THE OBEDIENT

Daily, though no ears attended,
Did my prayers arise.
Daily, though no fire descended,
Did I sacrifice.
Though my darkness did not lift,
Though I faced no lighter odds,
Though the Gods bestowed no gift,
  None the less,
None the less, I served the Gods!

A DRIFTER OFF TARENTUM

He from the wind-bitten North with ship and companions
  descended,
Searching for eggs of death spawned by invisible hulls.
Many he found and drew forth. Of a sudden the fishery
  ended
In flame and a clamourous breath known to the
  eye-pecking gulls.

DESTROYER IN COLLISION

For Fog and Fate no charm is found
To lighten or amend.
I, hurrying to my bride, was drowned –
Cut down by my best friend.

CONVOY ESCORT

I was a shepherd to fools
Causelessly bold or afraid.
They would not abide by my rules.
Yet they escaped. For I stayed.

UNKNOWN FEMALE CORPSE

Headless, lacking foot and hand,
Horrible I come to land.
I beseech all women's sons
Know I was a mother once.

RAPED AND REVENGED

One used and butchered me: another spied
Me broken – for which thing an hundred died.
So it was learned among the heathen hosts
How much a freeborn woman's favour costs.

SALONIKAN GRAVE

I have watched a thousand days
Push out and crawl into night
Slowly as tortoises.
Now I, too, follow these.
It is fever, and not the fight –
Time, not battle, – that slays.

THE BRIDEGROOM

Call me not false, beloved,
If, from thy scarce-known breast
So little time removed,
In other arms I rest.

For this more ancient bride,
Whom coldly I embrace,
Was constant at my side
Before I saw thy face.

Our marriage, often set –
By miracle delayed –
At last is consummate,
And cannot be unmade.

Live, then, whom Life shall cure,
Almost, of Memory,
And leave us to endure
Its immortality.

V.A.D. (MEDITERRANEAN)

Ah, would swift ships had never been, for then we ne'er
   had found,

These harsh Aegean rocks between, this little virgin
   drowned,
Whom neither spouse nor child shall mourn, but men she
   nursed through pain
And – certain keels for whose return the heathen look in
   vain.

ACTORS
On a Memorial Tablet in Holy Trinity Church,
Stratford-on-Avon

We counterfeited once for your disport
Men's joy and sorrow: but our day has passed.
We pray you pardon all where we fell short –
Seeing we were your servants to this last.

JOURNALISTS
On a Panel in the Hall of the Institute of Journalists

We have served our day.

Rudyard Kipling

A Death-Bed

'This is the State above the Law.
The State exists for the State alone.'
[*This is a gland at the back of the jaw,*
And an answering lump by the collar-bone.]

Some die shouting in gas or fire;
Some die silent, by shell and shot.
Some die desperate, caught on the wire;
Some die suddenly. This will not.

'Regis suprema voluntas Lex'
[*It will follow the regular course of – throats.*]
Some die pinned by the broken decks,
Some die sobbing between the boats.

Some die eloquent, pressed to death
By the sliding trench as their friends can hear.
Some die wholly in half a breath.
Some – give trouble for half a year.

'There is neither Evil nor Good in life.
Except as the needs of the State ordain.'
[*Since it is rather too late for the knife,*
All we can do is mask the pain.]

Some die saintly in faith and hope –
Some die thus in a prison-yard –
Some die broken by rape or the rope;
Some die easily. This dies hard.

'I will dash to pieces who bar my way.
Woe to the traitor! Woe to the weak!'
[Let him write what he wishes to say.
It tires him out if he tries to speak.]

Some die quietly. Some abound
In loud self-pity. Others spread
Bad morale through the cots around . . .
This is a type that is better dead.

'The war was forced on me by my foes.
All that I sought was the right to live.'
[Don't be afraid of a triple dose;
The pain will neutralize half we give.

Here are the needles. See that he dies
While the effects of the drug endure . . .
What is the question he asks with his eyes? –
Yes, All-Highest, to God, be sure.]

Rudyard Kipling

Gethsemane

The Garden called Gethsemane
In Picardy it was,
And there the people came to see
The English soldiers pass.
We used to pass — we used to pass
Or halt, as it might be,
And ship our masks in case of gas
Beyond Gethsemane.

The Garden called Gethsemane,
It held a pretty lass,
But all the time she talked to me
I prayed my cup might pass.
The officer sat on the chair,
The men lay on the grass,
And all the time we halted there
I prayed my cup might pass.

It didn't pass — it didn't pass —
It didn't pass from me.
I drank it when we met the gas
Beyond Gethsemane!

Rudyard Kipling

The Mother's Son

I have a dream — a dreadful dream
A dream that is never done,
I watch a man go out of his mind,
And he is My Mother's Son.
They pushed him into a Mental Home,
And that is like the grave:
For they do not let you sleep upstairs,
And you're not allowed to shave.
And it was not disease or crime
Which got him landed there,
But because They laid on My Mother's Son
More than a man could bear.
What with noise, and fear of death,
Waking, and wounds and cold,
They filled the Cup for My Mother's Son
Fuller than it could hold.
They broke his body and his mind
And yet They made him live,
And They asked more of My Mother's Son
Than any man could give.
For, just because he had not died,
Nor been discharged nor sick,
They dragged it out with my Mother's Son
Longer than he could stick . . .
And no one knows when he'll get well
So, there he'll have to be:
And, 'spite of the beard in the looking-glass,
I know that man is me!

Rudyard Kipling

War Girls

There's the girl who clips your ticket for the train,
And the girl who speeds the lift from floor to floor,
There's the girl who does a milk-round in the rain,
And the girl who calls for orders at your door.
Strong, sensible, and fit,
They're out to show their grit,
And tackle jobs with energy and knack.
No longer caged and penned up,
They're going to keep their end up
Till the khaki soldier boys come marching back.

There's the motor girl who drives a heavy van,
There's the butcher girl who brings your joint of meat,
There's the girl who cries 'All fares, please!' like a man,
And the girl who whistles taxis up the street.
Beneath each uniform
Beats a heart that's soft and warm,
Though of canny mother-wit they show no lack;
But a solemn statement this is,
They've no time for love and kisses
Till the khaki soldier-boys come marching back.

Jessie Pope

For the Fallen

With proud thanksgiving, a mother for her children,
England mourns for her dead across the sea.
Flesh of her flesh they were, spirit of her spirit,
Fallen in the cause of the free.

Solemn the drums thrill; Death august and royal
Sings sorrow up into immortal spheres,
There is music in the midst of desolation
And a glory that shines upon our tears.

They went with songs to the battle, they were young,
Straight of limb, true of eye, steady and aglow.
They were staunch to the end against odds uncounted;
They fell with their faces to the foe.

They shall grow not old, as we that are left grow old:
Age shall not weary them, nor the years condemn.
At the going down of the sun and in the morning
We will remember them.

They mingle not with their laughing comrades again;
They sit no more at familiar tables of home;
They have no lot in our labour of the day-time;
They sleep beyond England's foam.

But where our desires are and our hopes profound,
Felt as a well-spring that is hidden from sight,
To the innermost heart of their own land they are known
As the stars are known to the Night;

As the stars that shall be bright when we are dust,
Moving in marches upon the heavenly plain;
As the stars that are starry in the time of our darkness,
To the end, to the end, they remain.

Laurence Binyon

Belgium

La Belgique ne regrette rien
Not with her ruined silver spires,
Not with her cities shamed and rent,
Perish the imperishable fires
That shape the homestead from the tent.

Wherever men are staunch and free,
There shall she keep her fearless state,
And homeless, to great nations be
The home of all that makes them great.

Edith Wharton

Spring in War-Time

I feel the spring far off, far off,
The faint, far scent of bud and leaf –
Oh, how can spring take heart to come
To a world in grief,
Deep grief?

The sun turns north, the days grow long,
Later the evening star grows bright –
How can the daylight linger on
For men to fight,
Still fight?

The grass is waking in the ground,
Soon it will rise and blow in waves –
How can it have the heart to sway
Over the graves,
New graves?

Under the boughs where lovers walked
The apple-blooms will shed their breath –
But what of all the lovers now
Parted by Death,
Grey Death?

Sara Teasdale

The War Films

O living pictures of the dead,
O songs without a sound,
O fellowship whose phantom tread
Hallows a phantom ground –
How in a gleam have these revealed
The faith we had not found.

We have sought God in a cloudy Heaven,
We have passed by God on earth:
His seven sins and his sorrows seven,
His wayworn mood and mirth,
Like a ragged cloak have hid from us
The secret of his birth.

Brother of men, when now I see
The lads go forth in line,
Thou knowest my heart is hungry in me
As for thy bread and wine;
Thou knowest my heart is bowed in me
To take their death for mine.

Henry Newbolt

Servitude

If it were not for England, who would bear
This heavy servitude one moment more?
To keep a brothel, sweep and wash the floor
Of filthiest hovels were noble to compare
With this brass-cleaning life. Now here, now there
Harried in foolishness, scanned curiously o'er
By fools made brazen by conceit, and store
Of antique witticisms thin and bare.

Only the love of comrades sweetens all,
Whose laughing spirit will not be outdone.
As night-watching men wait for the sun
To hearten them, so wait I on such boys
As neither brass nor Hell-fire may appal,
Nor guns, nor sergeant-major's bluster and noise.

Ivor Gurney

Photographs

(*To Two Scots Lads*)
Lying in dug-outs, joking idly, wearily;
  Watching the candle guttering in the draught;
Hearing the great shells go high over us, eerily
  Singing; how often have I turned over, and laughed

With pity and pride, photographs of all colours,
  All sizes, subjects: khaki brothers in France;
Or mother's faces worn with countless dolours;
  Or girls whose eyes were challenging and must dance,

Though in a picture only, a common cheap
  Ill-taken card; and children − frozen, some
(Babies) waiting on Dicky-bird to peep
  Out of the handkerchief that is his home

(But he's so shy!) And some with bright looks, calling
  Delight across the miles of land and sea,
That not the dread of barrage suddenly falling
  Could quite blot out—not mud nor lethargy.

Smiles and triumphant careless laughter. O
  The pain of them, wide Earth's most sacred things!
Lying in dug-outs, hearing the great shells slow
  Sailing mile-high, the heart mounts higher and sings.

But once – O why did he keep that bitter token
  Of a dead Love? – that boy, who, suddenly moved,
Showed me, his eyes wet, his low talk broken,
  A girl who better had not been beloved.

Ivor Gurney

To His Love

He's gone, and all our plans
Are useless indeed.
We'll walk no more on Cotswold
Where the sheep feed
Quietly and take no heed.

His body that was so quick
Is not as you
Knew it, on Severn river
Under the blue
Driving our small boat through.

You would not know him now . . .
But still he died
Nobly, so cover him over
With violets of pride
Purple from Severn side.

Cover him, cover him soon!
And with thick-set
Masses of memoried flowers –
Hide that red wet
Thing I must somehow forget.

Ivor Gurney

First Time In

After the dread tales and red yarns of the Line
Anything might have come to us; but the divine
Afterglow brought us up to a Welsh colony
Hiding in sandbag ditches, whispering consolatory
Soft foreign things. Then we were taken in
To low huts candle-lit, shaded close by slitten
Oilsheets, and there but boys gave us kind welcome,
So that we looked out as from the edge of home,
Sang us Welsh things, and changed all former notions
To human hopeful things. And the next day's guns
Nor any Line-pangs ever quite could blot out
That strangely beautiful entry to war's rout;
Candles they gave us, precious and shared over-rations –
Ulysses found little more in his wanderings without doubt.
'David of the White Rock', the 'Slumber Song' so soft, and
    that
Beautiful tune to which roguish words by Welsh pit boys
Are sung – but never more beautiful than here under the
    guns' noise.

Ivor Gurney

War Mothers

There is something in the sound of drum and fife
That stirs all the savage instincts into life.

In the old times of peace we went our ways,
Through proper days
Of little joys and tasks. Lonely at times,
When from the steeple sounded wedding chimes,
Telling to all the world some maid was wife –
But taking patiently our part in life
As it was portioned us by Church and State,
Believing it our fate.
  Our thoughts all chaste
Held yet a secret wish to love and mate
  Ere youth and virtue should go quite to waste.
But men we criticised for lack of strength,
And kept them at arm's length.
Then the war came –
The world was all aflame!
The men we had thought dull and void of power
Were heroes in an hour.
He who had seemed a slave to petty greed
Showed masterful in that great time of need.
He who had plotted for his neighbour's pelf,
Now for his fellows offers up himself.
And we were only women, forced by war
To sacrifice the things worth living for.

Something within us broke,
  Something within us woke,
    The wild cave-woman spoke.

When we heard the sound of drumming,
　As our soldiers went to camp,
　Heard them tramp, tramp, tramp;
As we watched to see them coming,
　And they looked at us and smiled
　(Yes, looked back at us and smiled),
As they filed along by hillock and by hollow,
　Then our hearts were so beguiled
　That, for many and many a day,
　We dreamed we heard them say,
'Oh, follow, follow, follow!'
　And the distant, rolling drum
　Called us 'Come, come, come!'
　Till our virtue seemed a thing to give away.

War had swept ten thousand years away from earth.
　We were primal once again.
　There were males, not modern men;
We were females meant to bring their sons to birth.
　And we could not wait for any formal rite,
　We could hear them calling to us, 'Come to-night;
For to-morrow, at the dawn,
We move on!'
　And the drum
　Bellowed, 'Come, come, come!'
And the fife
Whistled, 'Life, life, life!'

So they moved on and fought and bled and died;
Honoured and mourned, they are the nation's pride.
We fought our battles, too, but with the tide
Of our red blood, we gave the world new lives.
Because we were not wives

We are dishonoured. Is it noble, then,
To break God's laws only by killing men
To save one's country from destruction?
We took no man's life but gave our chastity,
And sinned the ancient sin
To plant young trees and fill felled forests in.

Oh, clergy of the land,
Bible in hand,
All reverently you stand,
   On holy thoughts intent
   While barren wives receive the sacrament!
Had you the open visions you could see
   Phantoms of infants murdered in the womb,
   Who never knew a cradle or a tomb,
Hovering about these wives accusingly.

Bestow the sacrament! Their sins are not well known –
Ours to the four winds of the earth are blown.

Ella Wheeler Wilcox

Dawn on the Somme

Last night rain fell over the scarred plateau
And now from the dark horizon, dazzling, flies
Arrow on fire-plumed arrow to the skies
Shot from the bright arc of Apollo's bow;
And from the wild and writhen waste below,
From flashing pools and mounds lit one by one,
O is it mist or are these companies
Of morning heroes who arise, arise
With thrusting arms, with limbs and hair aglow
Toward the risen god, upon whose brow
Burns the gold laurel of all victories,
Hero and hero's god, th' invincible Sun?

Robert Nichols

Battery Moving Up to a New Position from Rest Camp: Dawn

Not a sign of life we rouse
In any square close-shuttered house
That flanks the road we amble down
Toward far trenches through the town.

The dark, snow-slushy, empty street . . .
Tingle of frost in brow and feet . . .
Horse-breath goes dimly up like smoke.
No sound but the smacking stroke

Of a sergeant flings each arm
Out and across to keep him warm,
And the sudden splashing crack
Of ice-pools broken by our track.

More dark houses, yet no sign
Of life . . . An axle's creak and whine . . .
The splash of hooves, the strain of trace . . .
Clatter: we cross the market place.

Deep quiet again, and on we lurch
Under the shadow of a church:
Its tower ascends, fog-wreathed and grim;
Within its aisles a light burns dim . . .

When, marvellous! from overhead,
Like abrupt speech of one deemed dead,
Speech-moved by some Superior Will,
A bell tolls thrice and then is still.

And suddenly I know that now
The priest within, with shining brow,
Lifts high the small round of the Host.
The server's tingling bell is lost

In clash of the greater overhead.
Peace like a wave descends, is spread,
While watch the peasants' reverent eyes . . .

The bell's boom trembles, hangs, and dies.

O people who bow down to see
The Miracle of Calvary,
The bitter and the glorious,
Bow down, bow down and pray for us.

Once more our anguished way we take
Toward our Golgotha, to make
For all our lovers sacrifice.
Again the troubled bell tolls thrice.

And slowly, slowly, lifted up
Dazzles the overflowing cup.

O worshipping, fond multitude,
Remember us too, and our blood.

Turn hearts to us as we go by,
Salute those about to die,
Plead for them, the deep bell toll:
Their sacrifice must soon be whole.

Entreat you for such hearts as break
With the premonitory ache
Of bodies, whose feet, hands, and side,
Must soon be torn, pierced, crucified.

Sue for them and all of us
Who the world over suffer thus,
Who have scarce time for prayer indeed,
Who only march and die and bleed.

* * * * *

The town is left, the road leads on,
Bluely glaring in the sun,
Toward where in the sunrise gate
Death, honour, and fierce battle wait.

Robert Nichols

The Cenotaph

Not yet will those measureless fields be green again
Where only yesterday the wild sweet blood of wonderful
    youth was shed;
There is a grave whose earth must hold too long, too
    deep a stain,
Though for ever over it we may speak as proudly as we
    may tread.
But here, where the watchers by lonely hearths from the
    thrust of an inward sword have more slowly bled,
We shall build the Cenotaph: Victory, winged, with Peace,
    winged too, at the column's head.
And over the stairway, at the foot – oh! here, leave
    desolate, passionate hands to spread
Violets, roses, and laurel with the small sweet twinkling
    country things
Speaking so wistfully of other Springs
From the little gardens of little places where son or
    sweetheart was born and bred.
In splendid sleep, with a thousand brothers
To lovers – to mothers
Here, too, lies he:
Under the purple, the green, the red,
It is all young life: it must break some women's hearts
    to see
Such a brave, gay coverlet to such a bed!
Only, when all is done and said,
God is not mocked and neither are the dead.
For this will stand in our Market-place –
Who'll sell, who'll buy
(Will you or I
Lie each to each with the better grace)?

While looking into every busy whore's and huckster's
   face
As they drive their bargains, is the Face
Of God: and some young, piteous, murdered face.

Charlotte Mew

Soldier from the Wars Returning

Soldier from the wars returning,
Spoiler of the taken town,
Here is ease that asks not earning;
Turn you in and sit you down.

Peace is come and wars are over,
Welcome you and welcome all,
While the charger crops the clover
And his bridle hangs in stall.

Now no more of winters biting,
Filth in trench from fall to spring,
Summers full of sweat and fighting
For the Kesar or the King.

Rest you, charger, rust you, bridle;
Kings and kesars, keep your pay;
Soldier, sit you down and idle
At the inn of night for aye.

A.E. Housman

Bombardment

The Town has opened to the sun.
Like a flat red lily with a million petals
She unfolds, she comes undone.

A sharp sky brushes upon
The myriad glittering chimney-pots
As she gently exhales to the sun.

Hurrying creatures run
Down the labyrinth of the sinister flower.
What is it they shun?

A dark bird falls from the sun.
It curves in a rush to the heart of the vast
Flower: the day has begun.

D.H. Lawrence

Magpies in Picardy

The magpies in Picardy
Are more than I can tell.
They flicker down the dusty roads
And cast a magic spell
On the men who march through Picardy,
Through Picardy to hell.

(The blackbird flies with panic,
The swallow goes with light,
The finches move like ladies,
The owl floats by at night;
But the great and flashing magpie
He flies as artists might.)

A magpie in Picardy
Told me secret things —
Of the music in white feathers,
And the sunlight that sings
And dances in deep shadows —
He told me with his wings.

(The hawk is cruel and rigid,
He watches from a height;
The rook is slow and sombre,
The robin loves to fight;
But the great and flashing magpie
He flies as lovers might.)

He told me that in Picardy,
An age ago or more,
While all his fathers still were eggs,

These dusty highways bore
Brown, singing soldiers marching out
Through Picardy to war.

He said that still through chaos
Works on the ancient plan,
And two things have altered not
Since first the world began –
The beauty of the wild green earth
And the bravery of man.

(For the sparrow flies unthinking
And quarrels in his flight;
The heron trails his legs behind,
The lark goes out of sight;
But the great and flashing magpie
He flies as poets might.)

T.P. Cameron Wilson

Song of Amiens

Lord! How we laughed in Amiens!
For here were lights, and good French drink,
And Marie smiled at everyone,
And Madeleine's new blouse was pink,
And Petite Jeanne (who always runs)
Served us so charmingly, I think
That we forgot the unsleeping guns.

Lord! How we laughed in Amiens!
Till through the talk there flashed the name
Of some great man we left behind.
And then a sudden silence came,
And even Petite Jeanne (who runs)
Stood still to hear, with eyes aflame,
The distant mutter of the guns.

Ah! How we laughed in Amiens!
For there were useless things to buy,
Simply because Irene, who served,
Had happy laughter in her eye;
And Yvonne, bringing sticky buns,
Cared nothing that the eastern sky
Was lit with flashes from the guns.

And still we laughed in Amiens,
As dead men laughed a week ago.
What cared we if in Delville Wood
The splintered trees saw hell below?

We cared . . . We cared . . . But laughter runs
The cleanest stream a man may know
To rinse him from the taint of guns.

T.P. Cameron Wilson

During the Bombardment

What did we know of birds?
Though the wet woods rang with their blessing,
And the trees were awake and aware with wings,
And the little secrets of mirth, that have no words,
Made even the brambles chuckle, like baby things
Who find their toes too funny for any expressing.

What did we know of flowers?
Though the fields were gay with their flaming
Poppies, like joy itself, burning the young green
    maize,
And spreading their crinkled petals after the showers –
Cornflower vieing with mustard; and all the three
    of them shaming
The tired old world with its careful browns and
    greys.

What did we know of summer,
The larks, and the dusty clover,
And the little furry things that were busy and starry-
    eyed?
Each of us wore his brave disguise, like a mummer,
Hoping that no one saw, when the shells came over,
The little boy who was funking – somewhere inside!

T.P. Cameron Wilson

Achilles in the Trench

I saw a man this morning
Who did not wish to die
I ask, and cannot answer,
If otherwise wish I.

Fair broke the day this morning
Against the Dardanelles;
The breeze blew soft, the morn's cheeks
Were cold as cold sea-shells.

But other shells are waiting
Across the Aegean sea,
Shrapnel and high explosive,
Shells and hells for me.

O hell of ships and cities,
Hell of men like me,
Fatal second Helen,
Why must I follow thee?

Achilles came to Troyland
And I to Chersonese:
He turned from wrath to battle,
And I from three days' peace.

Was it so hard, Achilles,
So very hard to die?
Thou knewest and I know not —
So much the happier I.

I will go back this morning
From Imbros over the sea;
Stand in the trench, Achilles,
Flame-capped, and shout for me.

Patrick Shaw-Stewart

Signals

The hot wax drips from the flares
On the scrawled pink forms that litter
The bench where he sits; the glitter
Of stars is framed by the sandbags atop of the dug-out
    stairs.
And the lagging watch-hands creep;
And his cloaked mates murmur in sleep, –
Forms he can wake with a kick, –
And he hears, as he plays with the pressel-switch, the
    strapped receiver click
On his ear that listens, listens;
And the candle-flicker glistens
On the rounded brass of the switch-board where the red
    wires cluster thick.

Wires from the earth, from the air;
Wires that whisper and chatter
At night, when the trench-rats patter
And nibble among the rations and scuttle back to their lair;
Wires that are never at rest, –
For the linesmen tap them and test,
And ever they tremble with tone: –
And he knows from a hundred signals the buzzing call of
    his own,
The breaks and the vibrant stresses, –
The Z and the G and the S's
That call his hand to the answering key and his mouth to
    the microphone.

For always the laid guns fret
On the words that his mouth shall utter,
When rifle and Maxim stutter
And the rockets volley to starward from the spurting
  parapet;
And always his ear must hark
To the voices out of the dark, –
For the whisper over the wire,
From the bombed and the battered trenches where the
  wounded moan in the mire, –
For a sign to waken the thunder
Which shatters the night in sunder
With the flash of the leaping muzzles and the beat of
  battery-fire.

Gilbert Frankau

Eyes in the Air

Our guns are a league behind us, our target a mile below,
And there's never a cloud to blind us from the haunts of
  our lurking foe —
Sunk pit whence his shrapnel tore us, support-trench crest
  concealed,
As clear as the charts before us, his ramparts lie revealed.
His panicked watchers spy us, a droning threat in the void;
Their whistling shells outfly us — puff upon puff, deployed
Across the green beneath us, across the flanking grey,
In fume and fire to sheath us and baulk us of our prey.

  Before, beyond, above her,
  Their iron web is spun:
  Flicked but unsnared we hover,
  Edged planes against the sun:
  Eyes in the air above his lair,
  The hawks that guide the gun!

No word from earth may reach us, save, white against the
  ground,
The strips outspread to teach us whose ears are deaf to
  sound:
But down the winds that sear us, athwart our engine's shriek,
We send and know they hear us, the ranging guns we speak.
Our visored eyeballs show us their answering pennant, broke
Eight thousand feet below us, a whorl of flame-stabbed
  smoke
The burst that hangs to guide us, while numbed gloved
  fingers tap
From wireless key beside us the circles of the map.

Line target short or over
Come, plain as clock hands run,
Words from the birds that hover,
Unblinded, tail to sun;
Words out of air to range them fair,
From hawks that guide the gun!

Your flying shells have failed you, your landward guns
are dumb:
Since earth hath naught availed you, these skies be open!
Come,
Where, wild to meet and mate you, flame in their
beaks for breath,
Black doves! the white hawks wait you on the wind-
tossed boughs of death.
These boughs be cold without you, our hearts are
hot for this,
Our wings shall beat about you, our scorching breath
shall kiss;
Till, fraught with that we gave you, fulfilled of our
desire,
You bank too late to save you from biting beaks of fire

Turn sideways from your lover,
Shudder and swerve and run,
Tilt; stagger; and plunge over
Ablaze against the sun:
Doves dead in air, who clomb to dare
The hawks that guide the gun!

Gilbert Frankau

In the Morning

The firefly haunts were lighted yet,
As we scaled the top of the parapet;
But the east grew pale to another fire,
As our bayonets gleamed by the foeman's wire;
And the sky was tinged with gold and grey,
And under our feet the dead men lay,
Stiff by the loop-holed barricade;
Food of the bomb and the hand-grenade;
Still in the slushy pool and mud
Ah, the path we came was a path of blood,
When we went to Loos in the morning.

A little grey church at the foot of a hill,
With powdered glass on the window-sill
The shell-scarred stone and the broken tile,
Littered the chancel, nave, and aisle
Broken the altar and smashed the pyx,
And the rubble covered the crucifix;
This we saw when the charge was done,
And the gas-clouds paled in the rising sun,
As we entered Loos in the morning.

The dead men lay on the shell-scarred plain,
Where Death and the Autumn held their reign
Like banded ghosts in the heavens grey
The smoke of the powder paled away;
Where riven and rent the spinney trees
Shivered and shook in the sullen breeze,
And there, where the trench through the graveyard wound
The dead men's bones stuck over the ground
By the road to Loos in the morning.

The turret towers that stood in the air,
Sheltered a foeman sniper there
They found, who fell to the sniper's aim,
A field of death on the field of fame;
And stiff in khaki the boys were laid
To the sniper's toll at the barricade,
But the quick went clattering through the town,
Shot at the sniper and brought him down,
As we entered Loos in the morning.

The dead men lay on the cellar stair,
Toll of the bomb that found them there.
In the street men fell as a bullock drops,
Sniped from the fringe of Hulluch copse.
And the choking fumes of the deadly shell
Curtained the place where our comrades fell.
This we saw when the charge was done
And the east blushed red to the rising sun
In the town of Loos in the morning.

Patrick MacGill

We Shall Keep the Faith

Oh! you who sleep in Flanders Fields,
Sleep sweet — to rise anew!
We caught the torch you threw
And holding high, we keep the Faith
With All who died.

We cherish, too, the poppy red
That grows on fields where valor led;
It seems to signal to the skies
That blood of heroes never dies,
But lends a lustre to the red
Of the flower that blooms above the dead
In Flanders Fields.

And now the Torch and Poppy Red
We wear in honor of our dead.
Fear not that ye have died for naught;
We'll teach the lesson that ye wrought
In Flanders Fields.

Moina Michael

A Tribute*

Somewhere in France he fell,
Him, whom we loved so well.
Just how we cannot tell,
But this I know —
'Twas with a dauntless eye,
Fearless and head held high
In the way all heroes die,
Face to the foe.

Never himself he spared.
But with his men he dared.
All of their dangers shared.
Leader and friend;
Unselfish, kind and brave.
For others his life he gave.
Now in a soldier's grave.
Sleeps at the end.

Not his to funk or crawl,
When came his country's call.
Gladly he gave his all,
Welcomed the chance.
Treasured his memory
All through the years shall be.
Ah, but the heart of me,
Lies somewhere in France.

Ernest Melville

*Lt. W. L, killed in action July, 1917

Call of the Dead

Canna ye see them yet? – those laddies who marched away
With pipers playing brawly and kilts and ribbons gay,
With their upturned sunny faces, their laughter and their fun?
To think, O, God, 'twere mine to see them falling one by one!
They tackled the tasks that came their way; paid – to the
   limit paid.

Dinna ye hear them calling . . . above the bullet's whine?
List, and ye'll hear them calling, those comrade dead of
   mine.
Still are they carrying on, with the light of faith in their
   eyes,
With laughter and sun in their hearts to the heights of
   Paradise.
There at the hands of a kindly God I know that all is well
With the lads who quested to war, and joked when they
   found its hell.

Here at my post alone, where the sky is flaming red,
I vision them – I hear them call, that host of comrade
   dead.
Its gripping me and haunting me, aye by this thought
   obsessed,
That I want to go now, with those who were braves and
   best.
Now – when the road to the heavenly heights is thronged
   with soldier young,
Rather than wait for a tardy fate, and pass alone and
   unsung.

Ernest Melville

The Puzzle

Billy and I, we enlisted both in the same Scottish town,
Joined the same battalion and were sent to the same
  platoon.
Had never met before, but thrown together by chance;
We became the best of pals and drifted together to France.
Billy was only a youngster – just a rookie fresh from
  school;
Put his books away when he heard the call.
I'm – well, just a fool.
Life, with the years ahead was his, with every promise of
  fame;
Mine is a record of failure with none but myself to blame.

He was a mother's pride and joy – sunny-eyed, straight
  and clean;
I claim kin to none on earth; been all I shouldn't have
  been.
Billy, he was keen and bright, full of the zest of life;
I've played a losing game with Fate – just about sick of the
  strife.
I have roamed to ends of earth at the lure of a vagrant call;
Have seen the world and am satisfied. He –
  well hardly at all.
I've had my chance – didn't take it; didn't care if I passed
  away.
But Billy was young and ambitious. Billy wanted to stay.

Well, here I lie in hospital, where everything's
  clean and bright;
The doctor thinks in a week or two that I'll
  be quite allright.

But poor little Billy I left in France 'neath a wooden cross.
('Twas just like taking the gold away and
    sending back the dross.)
Do things happen in any old way – is everything
    left to chance?
Is this talk of Destiny and God only a bit of Romance?
Then why was Billy taken and me left here to rant?
I don't understand. Have tried to figure it out
– but I can't.

Ernest Melville

Fatigues

There's a certain hour of evening that I have
    come to dread,
It is the hour when decent folks are thinkin'
    of their bed;
But I'm sure to be goin' with a working-gang
    instead,
A-slitherin' through the mud and rain.
So we trudge along a labyrinth of never-endin'
    trench.
With heavies burstin' overhead (Lor' they do
    make a stench.
Say, this wouldn't be a bad place to come
    walkin' with a wench –
It looks just like a bloomin' country lane).

It isn't always fightin' – this holdin' of the line.
For we spend a lot of labour haulin' sandbags
    out a mine –
By the number that comes up you'd think
    they'd reached the Rhine,
(Ain't this bloomin' war never goin' to end?)
We heave them o'er the parapet, Lor' how
    those boys can swear,
When Fritz sends o'er a whizbang or a nasty
    flick'ring glare,
Or gets his ticker goin' – we sure do get a
    scare,

When first I joined the army I thought 'twould
    be sublime

To be fightin' for my country in France's
   sunny clime,
But instead I am workin' for the R. E.'s half
   the time
Like any bloomin' navvy with a spade.
We do all the work it seems, the R. E's get
   the pay.
They get three shillin's and us — a measly bob
   a day.
Lor' in the British army don't they have a
   funny way, —
Oh, the miles and miles of trenches that
   I've made.

But while we're here we plug away and do our
   very best;
The thing that keeps us goin' is the rumour
   of a rest —
Alas! that now has got to be an ancient sort
   of jest.
(Even the grim god of war has got to have
   his fun.)
It's a long, long lane, you know, that has no
   end in sight.
And we'll come marchin' homeward some
   morning's dawning light;
So hustle, boys, get busy, and work with all
   your might,
Every little bit helps to down the Hun.

Ernest Melville

When it's Over

'Young soldier, what will you be
When it's all over?'
'I shall get out and across the sea,
Where land's cheap and a man can thrive.
I shall make money. Perhaps I'll wive
In a place where there's room for a family.
        I'm a bit of a rover.'

'Young soldier, what will you be
At the last "Dismiss"?'
'Bucked to get back to old Leicester Square,
Where there's good champagne and a glad eye winking,
And no more "Verey Lights" damnably blinking
Their weary, dreary, white-eyed stare.
I'll be out of this.'

'Young soldier, what will you be
When they sign the peace?'
'Blowed if I know; perhaps I shall stick it.
The job's all right if you take it steady.
After all, somebody's got to be ready,
And tons of the blighters 'll get their ticket.
        Wars don't cease.'

'Young soldier, what will you be
At the day's end?'
'Tired's what I'll be. I shall lie on the beach
Of a shore where the rippling waves just sigh,
And listen and dream and sleep and lie
Forgetting what I've had to learn and teach
        And attack and defend.'

'Young soldier, what will you be
When you're next a-bed?'
'God knows what; but it doesn't matter,
For whenever I think, I always remember
The Belgians massacred that September,
And England's pledge and the rest seems chatter.
        What if I *am* dead?'

'Young soldier, what will you be
When it's all done?'
'I shall come back and live alone
On an English farm in the Sussex Weald,
Where the wounds in my mind will be slowly sealed,
And the graves in my heart will be overgrown;
        And I'll sit in the sun.'

'Young soldier, what will you be
At the "Last Post"?'
'Cold, cold in the tender earth,
A cold body in foreign soil;
But a happy spirit fate can't spoil,
And an extra note in the blackbird's mirth
        From a khaki ghost.'

Max Plowman

Cha Till Maccruimein

Departure of the 4th Camerons

The pipes in the streets were playing bravely,
The marching lads went by,
With merry hearts and voices singing
My friends marched out to die;
But I was hearing a lonely pibroch
Out of an older war,
'Farewell, farewell, farewell, MacCrimmon,
MacCrimmon comes no more.'

And every lad in his heart was dreaming
Of honour and wealth to come,
And honour and noble pride were calling
To the tune of the pipes and drum;
But I was hearing a woman singing
On dark Dunvegan shore,
'In battle or peace, with wealth or honour,
MacCrimmon comes no more.'

And there in front of the men were marching,
With feet that made no mark,
The grey old ghosts of the ancient fighters
Come back again from the dark;
And in front of them all MacCrimmon piping
A weary tune and sore,
'On the gathering day, for ever and ever,
MacCrimmon comes no more.'

E.A. Mackintosh

Index of First Lines